The AUSTRALIAN CONSTITUTION as it is ACTUALLY WRITTEN

The AUSTRALIAN CONSTITUTION as it is ACTUALLY WRITTEN

By

Graham L Paterson

Strategic Book Publishing and Rights Co.

Strategic Book Publishing & Rights Co. LLC
USA | Singapore
www.sbpra.com

For information about special discounts for bulk purchases, please contact Strategic Book Publishing and Rights Co. Special Sales, at bookorder@sbpra.net.

ISBN: 978-1-63135-842-5

DEDICATION

This book is dedicated to Salvatore Ganci, and the Community Law and Resources Association of Victoria, who were instrumental in its creation.

The book is also dedicated to anyone who has a genuine concern for the integrity of our Australian Governmental and legal system. Australia's primary law, the British Act we currently use as our Constitution, has never been applied as it is actually written.

As long as we continue to use this British Act as our Constitution, Australia cannot be an independent nation.

And finally, this book is dedicated to everyone who has a passionate and enduring desire to achieve Australia's rightful and proper place, as a truly sovereign and independent nation.

That will only happen when the people of Australia agree to write their own Australian Constitution, and proclaim it as being "by the people, for the people, and of the people."

Change the way people think and you change the future

Unknown

If your actions inspire other to dream more, learn more, do more and become more, you are a leader.

John Quincy Adams

FOREWORD

This book started off purely as a program of lessons. It turned out to be only the second book written in the last 114 years to analyse every Clause, Chapter and Section of the British Act used to create the Commonwealth of Australia. In actual fact, this historical book is a political and legal first, as it looks at Australia's Constitution in an honest and objective way, according to the words as they are actually written, and possibly more importantly, from today's perspective.

In 1901, Dr. John Quick and a barrister, Robert Garran, wrote their monumental volume, "The Annotated Constitution of the Commonwealth of Australia". It took them a thousand and eight pages to try and explain the Constitution in relation to the culture and legal concepts of the nineteenth century thinking. That thinking automatically enshrined the Westminster system of government that was developed over the centuries in Britain. The fact that the Westminster system is not mentioned in the Australian Constitution, or referred to in any way, did not present a stumbling block to these two venerable authors. Then as now, the Australian Constitution is purely seen as a legal document, a document written mainly by lawyers, with the intention that it should only be used and interpreted by lawyers.

The original lessons were aimed at teaching high school students about the British Act of 1900 that is still used today as the Australian Constitution, but the book you now have in front of you, has evolved to encompass a much wider audience.

A nation's Constitution, however, does represent the primary law of the country, and therefore affects and applies to every person, native-born or resident. If we accept this proposition as a fact, then by any logical and rational argument, the people of the nation should be able to read and understand what this "primary law" says, and to find out how it impacts on their lives.

It is a common cliché that "Ignorance of the law is no excuse", but when it comes to the "primary law" of Australia, it wouldn't be far wrong to say that ninety eight percent of the population is totally ignorant of what this Constitution actually says. And that would include many in the legal profession. I would even go as far as to say, without much fear of contradiction, every politician currently in the Australian Parliament.

What prompted me to turn these lessons into a book was a matter of happenstance. As I was browsing the books in a second-hand shop, I found a beautifully bound copy of a book entitled, "A Familiar Exposition on the Constitution of the United States", by Professor Joseph Story. It was a 1992 Special edition of the book that was first published in 1840. The book is dedicated to the "Cause of Education – explaining the true nature, reasons and objects thereof, designed for the use of schools, libraries and general readers".

Although Mr. Story was a Professor of Law at the Harvard University, he has approached the US Constitution in the same way as I have approached the Australian Constitution – by taking the words as they are written, and in the way they would be understood by ordinary people.

As Mr. Story was much closer to the origin of the US Constitution, he would have had a better understanding of *the reasons and objects*" for what was written, compared to my more distant relationship with the Australian Constitution.

However, if one is going to write a law, and especially the "primary law" of a nation, it should be written as clearly and straight forward as possible. It should not have to rely in inferences, on unwritten conventions, on precedent, and nor should it include undefined entities and processes.

The following lessons, which are the bulk of this book, simply take an objective look at the words of this British Act as they are actually written. The original title of that Act was," The British Colony of the Commonwealth of Australia Constitution Act 1900 (UK)". We were a colony of Britain when this Act was proclaimed on the 1st of January 1901, but in 1907, the British Parliament changed Australia's status to that of a Dominion.

As every legally trained person knows, this Australian Constitution Act is the sole property of the British Parliament, and it is entirely in the hands of that parliament to determine the status of the Australian nation. Only Britain has the legal power to repeal this Act, and thereby declare Australia a truly independent nation. It then becomes the responsibility of the Australian people to create their own genuine and up to date constitution.

Until this is done, Australia will continue to remain a Dominion of Britain, no matter what the High Court of Australia says, or what anyone else may say, think or wish.

Alternatively, the Australian people can take matters into their own hands and unilaterally declare our Independence, by demanding the creation of our own Australian created constitution.

That action will not occur until the majority of the Australian people have been educated about the true nature of the antiquated, out of date, nineteenth century Act that is still used as our constitution. In reality, the Act is really nothing more than a contract between the then colonies and how they might share "power" with a centralised government of a Federated Australian Colony, a colony to be known then, and as it is today, the Commonwealth of Australia.

Graham L. Paterson
November 2014.

TEACHING PROGRAM
FOR THE CONSTITUTION

INTRODUCTION

As the Australian Constitution would normally be considered a "dry", uninteresting and difficult subject to teach to school children, let alone adults, the key to any success is finding a way to arouse curiosity.

One way this might be done is to shroud the document in 'mystery', in secrecy, in conspiracy, while emphasising that this document is the most important piece of paper in their lives, and that's why it has been kept 'hidden' for so long.

To build up suspense, it is probably best not to mention the term 'constitution' at the start, but to just talk about how we need to find out more about this very important 'piece of paper'.

To do that, the program would start with some early Australian history, after first finding out what the students know about the subject. Once their level of understanding is established, the teacher can pick out some pertinent aspects that will lead into the creation of that 'piece of paper'.

Those aspects would involve some British history and the early colonisation of Australia, mainly as a penal settlement. Ultimately, that colonisation led to the establishment of the various colonies. Without spending too much time on this early history, the formation of the colonies would be the significant starting point. The next step is in explaining how the colonies, operated, and how they were governed.

The emphasis here would be on the issue of "power" – who had it – who did it effect – how was it used – and why it is important in shaping the 'piece of paper'.

All this would tie in with the 'secrecy' surrounding the 'piece of paper', and why it is important that this has never been taught, or discussed in Australian schools. From there we could move into the 'conspiracy' aspects by dealing with the selection of the few prominent people who got together and drew up this important 'piece of paper'. The lessons would emphasise that democracy didn't have anything to with writing the 'piece of paper', in fact; the idea of democracy was of no interest at all. Most of these prominent people didn't want the people to have any involvement, and certainly no women or aborigines.

We would then talk about what these people were trying to achieve by drawing up this 'piece of paper'. In particular, the initial reaction to the potential threat they saw from Britain's long time enemies, France and Germany, who were spreading their influence into the Pacific. This would bring in the connection with Fiji and New Zealand, who were part of these early discussions for countering the threat. It is important to get all these actions in context, and especially the prevailing view that combining the colonies in Australia was seen as a way to make a safer and stronger colony of Britain. The 'piece of paper' never, at any time, had anything to do with separating Australia from Britain, and the British Monarchy.

A PROGRAM of LESSONS

TEACHER'S NOTES

The introduction provides an outline of the approach envisaged for this program The main idea is to try and get the students to ask questions, and then try to focus on these issues as a step by step 'investigation' into why and how we finished up with the "piece of paper" we now have.

We do need to go back to the beginning of the story if we are going to get a proper understanding about what we have, and what is the philosophy behind it. Only then are we in a position to pick out its weaknesses and see what can be changed, or preferably re-written, to make it a proper people's "piece of paper" for an independent Australia.

These notes are an attempt to develop a course on the Australian Constitution that could be taught at high-school, or upper primary school level. As the Introduction points out, it suggests one way a practical program might be implemented. The real start has to be with the teachers - they are the ones that have to be "educated" first – in the sense that the general knowledge about the Australian Constitution is very limited. And of course, they have to want to do it objectively and honestly - not uncritically accept the conventional version of events that tends to be promoted by the legal profession, and the government.

Any program of this nature needs the input and ideas of others – nothing should be "set in concrete" and we need to find the most effective way for people to gain an interest in this important subject.

By presenting this course as a complete package – it is possible the educational value might gain some wider support, and these lessons could lay the foundation for that support.

Something like this really must be a joint effort in exchanging ideas – these notes are one lot of ideas, but there must be others that could improve these, and help make the program better and more effective.

What it needs are people with - SECS - as is explained in the booklet - "SECS and the Art of Public Speaking". SECS stands for Sincerity - Enthusiasm - Confidence - and Simplicity - speaking a language your audience can understand, and presenting it with confidence and enthusiasm. SECS also happens to be the essence of good teaching.

The issue of a new Australian Constitution is very likely to come into prominence within the next 3 years, when the current Queen of England either dies or abdicates. The idea of introducing students to the Constitution is really a preparation for that event. If the students do acquire an interest in this "piece of paper", it is more than likely they will raise the subject with their parents.

It is probably not appropriate to go into detail about acts or laws that emanate from this "piece of paper", although some of those laws do serve to illustrate how this "piece of paper" has been manipulated over the years. Instead, we should try and focus on showing its weaknesses, and suggesting how our "piece of paper" can be made better. The initial concept of this course is to start with a brief history, which can lead us into looking at the culture and background of the creators. Once we get to that stage, the course would look at Australia's true legal status, and why the governments and High Courts, over the past 94 years, have tried to cover up Australia's lack of sovereignty and true independence.

The course concludes with a brief look at the political system in place, and a discussion of the electoral options used in Australia.

LESSON 1

Background

Tell the students they going to become detectives. Their task is to investigate the mystery surrounding the most important bit of paper in all their lives.

To be good detectives, we have to get all the evidence we can, and we do that by asking questions, and trying to find out what is true and what is false. We also need to go right back to the beginning of the story, and find out why things happened the way they did.

It is up to the students to ask questions any time something isn't clear, or it is something they don't understand. To be a proper detective we have to be sure of our facts.

Very few people know much about this 'piece of paper', how and why it was created, who really owns it, who really understands what the writing means, or even why it is so important.

It is important because, it affects everyone living in Australia, whether they are born here or whether they weren't – and that is a fact – a very true fact.

So, where did it come from?

This piece of paper is a part of British history, and it really came from a time many years ago. In fact, we could say it goes back several hundreds of years, but that's too long a story for us to investigate. To cut a long story short, maybe, we should just look at the main people this 'piece of paper' talks about.

The evidence we get from reading this document is that the Kings and Queens of England are, quite clearly, the most important people, as they are the ones in charge of everything.

Why are they in charge of everything? That's probably something we need to investigate because, this is Australia, and as far as we know, those Kings and Queens live in England, although they do visit us occasionally.

So, why is this piece of paper all about Kings and Queens?

The answer to that requires us to go back in British history to the year 1701. For many centuries, Britain had been ruled by various Kings or Queens, who assumed they had the power of God to do as they pleased. They claimed they sat on the throne by "divine right", even though that claim was sometimes based on treachery, intrigue and murder. Over the years, a lot of people started to object to the idea of "divine right", and it more or less came to a head in the year 1297. That's when the Barons, and other leading people in England, forced the then King to sign a document called, the Magna Carta.

What this document basically did was to create an early form of Parliament, by allowing the Barons to rule the nation along side the King. However, this didn't really work out all that well, and it took another few hundred years before the Parliament finally decided to take control of the system.

They did this in 1701 by drawing up a law called, "The Act of Settlement", which said the future Kings and Queens of England are only allowed to sit on the throne because Parliament lets them.

There was no more such thing as a "divine right," although the monarch (as the Kings and Queens are called) could be the nominal head of the Church of England.

What has Religion got to do with this?

That's a bit of a complicated question because, a lot of people are confused about the role of religion in the way a nation is governed. Theoretically, religion and government aren't supposed to get mixed up with each other, and a democratic government is supposed to guarantee religious freedom for people to worship according to their beliefs.

However, the Christian religion is based around the Ten Commandments, which are a reasonable set of rules for most people to live together in a civilised society, irrespective of their other beliefs.

For many centuries, Europe in particular, but many other parts of the world, has been dominated by the Catholic religion, and that included England. However, King Henry VIII had an argument with the Catholic Church because he wanted to divorce his then wife and marry another woman. That wasn't allowed at the time so, he decided to start his own church, which became known as the Church of England. There was a lot of fighting and blood spilt over this decision, but both the Church of England and the Catholic Church did survive in England.

It is this religious link to the British royalty that has allowed them to continue to exist by what is called, "the grace of God". That is quite different from "divine right", which implied they represented God on earth. The "grace of God" means they are there with God's permission, but that doesn't necessarily mean religion should be mixed up with the way a government works.

So, what has this got to do with Australia, and our "piece of paper"?

When Captain Cook claimed Australia for the British Empire way back in 1770, he claimed this 'newly discovered' land in the name of the King of England. The British subsequently decided to use this new land as a penal colony. They sent their first load of convicts to Sydney in 1788, and it is that event which Australia now commemorates as Australia Day, on the twentysixth of January each year.

Over the next sixty odd years Australia was divided into six separate colonies, with each being controlled by a Governor, appointed by the British government to represent the King. During that sixty year period, Britain had three Kings and a Queen, the last one being Queen Victoria, who reigned from 1837 to 1901.

To begin with, all the colonies were under the command of military people, but as the colonies developed, many people saw the opportunity for a successful future.

How the Colonies got their own "pieces of paper" given to them by Britain

English society has always been a very structured society, starting with the aristocracy, and later joined by the wealthy merchants, but all of them relying on the common people in maintaining everyone's place in the hierarchy. This type of thinking was directly imported into the fledgling Australian colonies, until eventually, the landowners and wealthy people wanted a say in how the colony was run. A lot of the common people were too busy just surviving to worry about these sorts of things, and besides, it never really occurred to the 'leaders' of the colonies to let those 'other people' get involved. Eventually, each of the colonies were given their own 'pieces of paper' by the British government in London. This spelled out the rules for the Governors to run the colony, in association with some of the more important and wealthier residents.

LESSON 2

The Threat

Our investigation has now determined how early Australia developed as a number of different colonies within the land mass of Australia. In those early days communication was very slow, and the vast bulk of transportation was done by sea. Each colony had its own supply of intrepid explorers, who tramped or rode through the rugged interior of their domains. Suddenly, Britain's once inhospitable penal colony came alight when large pasture lands were discovered, but the real spark that ignited things was the discovery of gold in Victoria. Bendigo and Ballarat were each a treasure chest, and the real potential value of this colonised land mass soon became apparent.

At the time, the tentacles of the British Empire encompassed the world, but Britain's long time European adversaries were also expanding their claims into the Asian Pacific region. Germany had laid claim to the northern part of New Guinea, the French had established themselves in New Caledonia, and the Dutch were well entrenched on the islands of what is now Indonesia. There was even a threat of a Russian invasion in 1885 which prompted the Cooktown Council in northern Queensland, to request an Officer and arms be sent from Brisbane.

There is a Memorial Plaque in Cooktown that reads –"A cannon (Cast in 1805) three cannon balls, two rifles and an Officer were sent", supposedly to thwart the "invasion".

It was obviously successful in "frightening" off the Russians, as the "invasion" didn't occur!

Although there had been a couple of other attempts to promote greater cooperation between the colonies, these came to nothing until Major General Sir Bevan Edwards presented a report in 1889 to counter the perceived threat. The report recommended a unified defence for the colonies.

The first real attempt to discuss coordination between the colonies

The first attempt to discuss some form of genuine coordination between the colonies took place at Tenterfield in New South Wales. It occurred on the 24th of October, 1889, and was largely convened by Sir Henry Parkes, the then Premier of New South Wales.

As the conference was initiated from the point of view of defending the British possessions in the Pacific region, both

Fiji and New Zealand were invited to attend. Each participating Colony agreed to send two representatives, a senior politician and a senior public servant. The New Zealand representatives made the conference, but the Fiji representatives arrived too late. In total, there were twelve men at the meeting.

The culture of the times

What was discussed at this meeting can be found in the archives, but for our "investigation" we need to take a closer look at the attitudes and background of these twelve representatives.

To start with, we need to ask what they represented. Obviously, they represented their respective colonies and the respective governments they served.

Most of us are familiar with the well known reason so many British people fought wars, took possession of lands and countries around the world, and raised the British flag. It was always done *"in the name of King and country."* Hence, the politicians and public servants in that day and age, all swore to serve allegiance to the King. There was never any oath required to serve, or act, on behalf of the people. Democracy was a virtually unknown concept, and democratic ideas tended to be treated with contempt, if they were ever raised at all.

Politicians in the colonial Parliaments

We now need to look at the attitudes, and thinking, of the people who were to be involved with writing our "piece of paper".

A bit of 'evidence' that is gathered from research is that in 1855, none of the colonial parliamentarians were paid. We also find that only men were allowed to nominate for Parliament. As these men would not be paid for making the laws of the colony, they would need to be wealthy if they were to take on the job. By the 1890's, the Premier of the colonies and the

Speaker in the Parliament did receive a salary, but the other politicians didn't.

Hence, the parliamentary system of the day was very much controlled by interests of the wealthier people in charge. There was relatively little concern for the issues affecting the majority of the people. This was in keeping with the British customs and traditions of the times. It was never considered that ordinary people should have a significant voice in government, but some people, if they qualified, were allowed to vote at elections. Unfortunately, these attitudes prevailed right through to the end of the century and into the early 1900's, and consequently, they have a direct bearing on the formulation of our "piece of paper" under 'investigation'.

The ordinary people

When we investigate the position involving the majority of the male and female population of the colonies at that time, we find the following facts; some of the colonies did allow certain men to have a vote, provided they qualified, and in the case of the wealthier people, they were granted multiple votes. As the largest majority of the male population did not qualify, they were excluded from the voting process, and virtually denied a voice in the parliamentary system. Thus, the qualified voters, and the elected politicians, had a mutual interest in looking after their position in the society, and ensuring it was maintained.

Education was not considered a necessity for most women, hence, their interest and involvement in politics was limited. The normal perception in those days was that a woman's place was in the home, but South Australia and Western Australia did allow some women a conditional vote at certain local elections. Of course, the aborigines were not considered a part of the political process, other than on a very limited scale in South Australia.

The follow up

The outcome of this first meeting in 1889 was to convene a larger meeting in 1891, to be attended by fortyfive delegates from the Australian colonies. These delegates comprised the colonial Premiers, other politicians and some public servants, plus representatives from New Zealand, but none from Fiji this time. It was at this 1891 meeting that the first draft of our "mysterious piece of paper" was created. A Tasmanian lawyer, Andrew Inglis Clark, wrote the initial outline, and this was later used as the basis for a final draft.

Extending the interest in Federation

As we have learnt from our investigation to date, interest in the idea of coordinating, or federating the colonies, arose almost entirely from the colonial politicians. There was very little public involvement. However, that interest lost momentum after Sir Henry Parkes' government was defeated in October 1891. Edmund Barton took up the responsibility for resurrecting the issue. Barton successfully broadened the interest in federation beyond the colonial Parliaments by appealing to the merchants of the Murray Valley area. This area straddled the borders on New South Wales, Victoria and South Australia, where each colony imposed their respective custom duty on goods crossing the borders. Barton's efforts resulted in the formation of fifteen branches of the Australian Federation League.

Eventually, a conference was initiated in August of 1893 at a place called Corowa, in the Riverina district. One of the aims of the conference was the development of our "piece of paper" into a draft Constitution for federating the Australian colonies.

A radical proposal

It was at this conference that Dr. John Quick came up with a quite radical proposal for the times. He suggested that each colony should pass a law calling for the election of representatives to attend a compulsory Constitutional Convention. That was radical enough, but he made it even more radical by proposing, that if our "piece of paper" could become an accepted draft for an Australian Constitution, it should be put to a referendum in each colony.

Proposing such a referendum was an unprecedented and profound departure from the political customs and concepts of the day. Dr. Quick certainly did not advocate anything like a universal vote for all the men, and he definitely did not countenance giving a vote to women.

This 'novel proposal', as it was then described, was eventually adopted by all the colonies except Queensland and Western Australia.

LESSON 3

Looking back at the 1891 Meeting

Modern day historians like to refer to the 1891 meeting as a Constitution Convention, but its motivation was really about setting up a system for better coordination between the colonies. Andrew Clark had spent time in the United States, and was familiar with the US Constitution. When he presented his ideas for cooperation between the colonies, it was based on the US experience of federating their colonies and forming a central government. This original "piece of paper" was to become the foundation for a future Australian federation.

What we need to understand about this document is that the colonial governments, and more particularly, the leading lawyer/politicians, were the people responsible for its development. Essentially, four people were mainly involved: Samuel Griffith from Queensland, Andrew Clark from Tasmania, Alfred Deakin from Victoria, and Charles Kingston from South Australia. Consequently, our "piece of paper" was always perceived as a legal document, which was written, primarily, from the experience and perspective of lawyers and politicians, of which many of the originators happened to be both.

Attitudes towards democracy

None of these four "eminent" people, or any of the other people involved, were at all interested in the concept of "democracy," as we understand it today. This can be proven from two examples recorded in the archives. The first example was the suggestion that the Governor General of the proposed central government be "elected" to the position, but only by the politicians. This was quickly shot down in flames as being *ultra democratic* and not worthy of consideration. The next example was the idea of submitting a draft Constitution to eligible voters, but that too was rejected in the interests of *"caution and tact"*.

The principles in developing our "piece of paper"

British politics, then and now are based on what is known as the "Westminster system". This is a system that has been developed over the centuries, and relies on a lot of ancient Charters that defined the fundamental concepts for governing a nation. Some of the principle Charters are: the Magna Carta of 1297: the Habeas Corpus Acts of 1640, 1679 and 1816: and the Bill of Rights of 1688 and 1689, along with many others. Britain does not have its own written Constitution to spell out the rules of how the government is allowed to operate. The British government is largely based on the traditional way things have operated in the past. Consequently, the Westminster system is almost entirely based on unwritten rules that are known as "conventions".

As both Australia, and a large part of the US, were originally "taken over" by British people, it was natural they would adopt the Westminster system as the basis for their governments.

This is despite the fact that the US is a republican system and Australia remains under the monarchial system. They both relied on the Westminster system for establishing their central governments.

The accepted principles for cooperation between the colonies

In the development of colonial Australia, each colony eventually became, more or less, autonomous self governing entities under the overall control of the British King or Queen, but in reality, the British government. Consequently, each colonial government considered themselves to be the holders of all political "power" within their respective borders. It was simply not conceivable that the mass of ordinary people could in any way, be in charge of the government. Of course, there were some people who thought otherwise, but such concepts were never even considered by those in authority, and would have been totally rejected anyway. Thus, when it came to the colonies discussing how to form a central government, the discussion concentrated on how the colonies would share some of their political "power" with this new entity.

The real meaning of "political power"

We often hear talk of "power" in respect to governments, the law, for officials and others in authority. Political parties always seek to gain "power" in Parliament by getting a majority of their candidates elected. When it is really examined, this "power" that most politicians seek is simply the ability to control people. Without people, there can be no such thing as "political power". While politicians dress up their desire for "power" by saying they are acting in the best interest of other people, those 'best interests' are the ones decided by the politicians and their political party.

Theoretically, a democratic society is supposed to be based on "rule of law", but which laws are made, how they are interpreted, and how they are used, really comes down to the way a society of people choose to live. In other words, it depends on what philosophy the people wish to accept, or choose if they are ever given the opportunity. When it is all set and done, a philosophy is simply a set of ideas of how people want to live their lives. To translate a philosophy into practice, one must first determine the policies that should apply before implementing a system. In a rational society, the prime purpose of that system should be to benefit the people. Unfortunately, most systems in place today are there to maintain the status quo for the benefit of the people "in power".

We will discuss the philosophic principles for our "piece of paper" in a later lesson.

Abolishing some Myths

There was never any discussion about Australia becoming a separate and independent country from Britain. The intention was that Australia would always remain a colony of the "mother country". Our evidence of this is the inclusion of the words, *"unite in one indissoluble Federal Commonwealth under the Crown ......"*

From the point of view of the colonies, they were the most important parts of the proposed arrangements for federation. The colonies saw the role of the central government as coordinating cooperation between the colonies, achieving uniformity in the laws and in defence, and in promoting commerce, both internally and externally. Essentially, the proposed federal Constitution was a business contract between the colonies and a central government.

Where do *"the people"* fit into this "contract"?

That is a very interesting question, particularly in view of what we know about the "founding father's" attitudes towards the general population. Despite the assumptions made by some people, the Australian Constitution is not a document focusing on "the people".

Unlike the US constitution, the Australian "piece of paper" does not proclaim, "We, the people ....", and neither does it define who it is really talking about when it commences, *"Whereas the people ...."*

Just which "people" do the "founding fathers" have in mind? According to the figures published for the referendums in 1899, only about fifteen percent of the population was allowed to vote, and that percentage would be reduced when multiple votes are taken into account. The actual percentage of eligible people who supported federation was around eleven percent of the total population. This does not make a strong argument for claiming *"Whereas the people .... have agreed to unite ...."*. It should also be noted that the fifteen percent excluded women, and virtually all of the rank and file people of the colonies. Nor did it include any aborigines.

So, despite what modern day people like to assume, it appears quite arrogant to speak on behalf of the eightyfive percent of the then population that had no say in the acceptance of the "piece of paper."

Our draft document was not written from the perspective of the people, it was written by the politicians and lawyers for their benefit. This can be clearly shown from the thirtynine provisions they included to allow Parliament to make changes without calling a referendum.

How does the Westminster system impact on Australia?

Although all the politicians of the 1800's were fully aware of the Westminster system of government, and the impact political parties had in politics, the reality of party existence was completely ignored in our "piece of paper". What was even more alarming was the absence of any mention of a Prime Minister, let alone the duties, responsibilities, and limits of authority associated with the position. Everyone knew the Prime Minister of Britain was the most powerful political figure in that country so, why wasn't this recognised in the draft document?

Apart from these two major omissions, there was another significant omission in disregarding the effect of 'conventions' that apply under the Westminster system. By ignoring the 'conventions' the creators of our "piece of paper" set up a system of government that really had little relationship to the way it was implemented. To give a couple of brief examples, the Governor General is declared the Commander in Chief of the Armed Forces, and with the authority to open and close Parliament at 'his' discretion. Also to withhold assent to any laws passed by Parliament, "at the Queen's pleasure". He can choose to take the *advice* from a Federal Executive Council, for *administering* the country in the name of the Queen.

Without a Prime Minister being included and defined in our "piece of paper," surely, the way it is written, must make the Governor General the most "powerful" man in Australia?

In fact, it makes the position into a totally dictatorial one that is backed by the military.

It seems rather strange that none of our legal fraternity have ever questioned the reality of the system set out in this alarming "piece of paper".

The 1897 Constitutional Convention

To get back to our "investigation", we find it took another six years before our "piece of paper" came back into the spotlight. It was largely through Barton's efforts to drum up support for federating the colonies that the resolutions from the Corowa meeting eventually became a reality in 1897. The proposed convention finally took place in Adelaide during March of that year. Each colony, except Queensland, agreed to attend, and apart from Western Australia, the other four colonies had gone along with the scheme to "elect" ten delegates. The research into the "election" process is somewhat difficult, but it seems the process finished up choosing mostly senior politicians and public servants. The Western Australian Premier appointed his selected representatives without bothering about an "election".

We shall examine the developments resulting from the 1897 Convention in our next Lesson.

LESSON 4

The investigative procedure

As we all know from watching TV, good detectives always ask a lot of questions in the hope of getting to the truth. That's what we have to do too. But finding the truth is not always straight forward or easy. It is an unfortunate fact that people who write about history, often create it according to the information they choose to use, or the information that is available. This is very much the case with the history surrounding our "piece of paper". A lot of the research we need to do is coloured by the views of the writer, and a lot of the information is based on selected facts that fit that point of view. That's why we have to be like real modern detectives, and look for every bit of evidence we can find, especially at the scene of the crime.

Although writing our "piece of paper" wasn't a criminal offence, we do need to look at the detail of how it came about. As a detective on this 'case', one probably wonders why it is important we have to try and understand all we can about these old dead people. It is important because, what they wrote over a hundred years ago very much affects us today. They wrote the primary law for Australia. All the other laws made since 1901, are supposed to be based on what those old dead people wrote.

Obviously, things have changed an awful lot since the 1890's, and the Australian people have seen fit to change this primary law only nine times in the last 114 years. On the other hand, the politicians and Judges, have changed this primary law, literally, thousands of times, in fact they have made so many changes that no one has kept count. We'll have to look at how and why they did this.

The 3 important factors of any investigation

When detectives investigate a case, they look for three principle things – motive – opportunity – and means.

And these are the three things we have to look for in our 'investigation'. We have looked at some of the motive for writing our "piece of paper", but what we have discovered so far, is not the full story. The opportunity came about with the threat from the other European nations, but when that faded, the politicians had to find another opportunity. Barton used the problems of the Murray Valley area as a replacement. Our 'investigation' now leads us to the 'means' – the way the "piece of paper" actually came into being.

The Means – the 1897 Convention

The 1897 convention was the vehicle used to finalise the drafting of our "piece of paper". This convention was a logical follow-up from the 1891 meeting that saw the initial draft for the "document". The 1897 convention was quite an involved affair, which took place over a period of twelve months. It started off in Adelaide in March of 1897, had a meeting in Sydney, and finished up in Melbourne by March the following year. The actual sittings were:

Adelaide session	10th April 1897 to 5th May
Sydney session	2nd Sept 1897 to 24th Sept
Melbourne session, and the longest one,	20th Jan 1898 to 13th March 1898

The five participating colonies, New South Wales, Victoria, Western Australia, South Australia and Tasmania, each sent along their ten representatives.

The population of all the colonies in 1897/8 was in excess of three million people, but only fifty of these people got to discuss what was to be written. There are quite extensive archival records of the extended discussions that took place before final agreement could be reached on drafting our "piece of paper." When we delve into the makeup of the subcommittee for drafting the wording of this all important "piece of paper", we find that all the members were lawyers. This does have an important bearing on what was written. The subcommittee was made up of three or four people, depending on which records are used. The people named were, Sir John Downer, Edmund Barton, Alfred Deakin and Richard O'Conner, all influential politician/lawyers, well versed in the Westminster system of government.

It is said that the Constitutions of the US, Canada and Switzerland were used for reference in creating the Australian "piece of paper". One significant event that was taken from the Swiss Constitution was the fact the Swiss introduced referendums in 1874. The concept of the Senate was taken from the US Constitution, but Britain also had an upper House in the form of the House of Lords. The influence of these other Constitutions is much less compared to the British concept of what was called, "responsible government".

Just what is "responsible government"?

"Responsible government" is an English conceptual theory that was supposed to define the responsibility of parliamentary representatives in respect of their actions, and to whom they are responsible. In part it was an ethical concept. For example, if a representative lied to Parliament, they would be dismissed. It was also believed that the representative was elected to represent the people of their area. These relatively quaint ideas were completely over run by party politics, which for the past couple of centuries has dominated the political process.

Although every one of the fifty delegates at the 1897 convention were fully aware of the existence and influence of political parties, they chose to completely ignore them when writing our "piece of paper". As this is a very important factor in our investigation, we will need to look into the ramifications of this omission, and why the theory of "responsible government' was apparently accepted in principle, but less so in practice.

This will be dealt with later, as our investigation continues.

The composition of the delegates to the Convention

In order to get an understanding about the background and attitudes of the delegates to the convention, we need to do the research on the people involved. There appears some conflict in the records, as one account says there were forty "elected" delegates and ten appointed delegates, but the attendance of the latter from Western Australia was sporadic, and this might account for a variation in numbers.

A record showing the background of the delegates, indicates there were fiftyfour in attendance, of which twentyseven were lawyers/politicians. In terms of their political background, the figures show the following: thirtyone delegates were sitting members of the Colonial Legislative Assemblies - eight were sitting members of the colonial Legislative Councils - fourteen were past members of the Assemblies and Councils - one delegate without either connection happened to be a Banker, Mr. J. T. Walker.

Thus, the makeup of this Convention would certainly appear to have a preference in maintaining the system of government that had contributed to their standing and prosperity.

Preparation for the Federation Referendum

Once a final draft was accepted, it was then necessary for each colony to legislate for the agreed referendum amongst their eligible voters. There was a well organised and fairly strong opposition to the idea of federation, particularly in New South Wales, (NSW) the most populous colony. The local press of the day called this opposition the "anti-Billites", and those in favour were the "Billites". Despite the strength of the "anti–Billites", they were not given a voice in either of the two conventions. The only way the NSW opposition could express their frustration was in the colonial Parliament. They were successful in having a motion passed that required a minimum of eighty thousand referendum votes in favour of federation. The Victorian and South Australian Parliaments followed suit, but stipulated smaller numbers, fifty thousand for Victoria and six thousand for South Australia.

At the time, both South Australia and Western Australia had legislated to allow some women to vote at local colonial elections. There is some question whether women voted in the referendum for the federation, but the other colonies did grant some women the right to vote in federal politics after the year of 1901.

Voter Qualifications

The qualifications for male voters varied between the colonies, and it also varied between the candidates for the existing two houses of the colonial governments. Some colonies had the members of their Legislative Councils appointed by the Governor without election, while others required the voters to have property and graduate education qualifications for that house. When voting for members of the larger Legislative Assembly, the voter qualifications were less stringent, but never the less, restrictive.

It is difficult to establish exactly who qualified to vote in the federation referendums. However, by 1897, there was a general acceptance in the colonies that males, who were British subjects and over the age of twentyone, could vote. To qualify, they had to have lived in the colony for twelve months, and resided in a particular electoral district for a minimum of six months. Another factor that needs to be taken into account was voting was not compulsory.

The first referendum

When the referendum was announced for the third and fourth of June 1898, both Queensland and Western Australia refused to take part. Despite this, the referendum went ahead in the four other colonies. Without the two largest parts of the Australian continent being involved, it is questionable as to what sort of federation could be achieved.

What question was asked at the referendum?

It is quite important for our investigation to find out what the voters were asked at the referendum. From a search of the internet the only example of the official papers issued to the voters is shown at http://www.timetoast.com/timelines/timeline-to-federation--14 the question asked of the voters was whether they wanted "union of the colonies, or disunion?" The papers implied that by voting for "union" they automatically accepted the "piece of paper" that had been drawn up on 'their behalf'. This "piece of paper" was to become the Constitution of Australia, once Queen Victoria had agreed and signed the document in England.

The results from this referendum in 1898 were:

NSW	For	71,595	Against	66.228
Victoria	For	100,520	Against	22,099
Sth Aust.	For	35,800	Against	17,320
Tasmania	For	11,798	Against	2,716
Total	For	219,712	Against	108,363

When NSW did not receive the required eighty thousand "Yes" votes the referendum was considered to be lost, and federation would not go ahead.

The 'secret' Premiers' conference

The loss at the referendum was a disappointing blow to the Premiers of the colonies, who had invested so much time and energy over the years. In an effort to win the support of the New South Wales and Queensland colonial Parliaments, the Premiers of NSW, Victoria, South Australia, Tasmania and Queensland, got together privately in January of 1899, to discuss and make changes to the draft Constitution. Some reports say the Western Australian Premier, John Forrest, attended this meeting, and others say he chose not to attend.

Over the next five days, the Premiers agreed to five changes for the benefit of New South Wales, and one change for Queensland. Among the changes was the decision to locate the future Australian national capital within New South Wales, but at least one hundred miles (one hundred and sixty kilometers) from Sydney. They also agreed the federal Parliament would only be required to return customs and excise revenue to the colonies for the first ten years of federation, rather than it being a permanent arrangement. The other decision made by the Premiers was to hold another referendum of the four colonies.

Second referendum: 1899

Approval for this second referendum still had to be obtained from the colonial Parliaments, and after more debate, this was obtained. The NSW upper house still insisted on the eighty thousand acceptance votes, and this was comfortably exceeded this second time around. The second referendum was held in Victoria, South Australia, New South Wales and Tasmania between April and July of 1899. This time, all four colonies agreed to federation with the required number of approval votes. Queensland delayed their referendum to see what happened in NSW, and the following September, Queenslanders endorsed federation by the narrowest of margins, with just over fiftyfour per cent voting 'yes'.

The results this time were as follows:

NSW	For	107 420	Against	82 741
Victoria	For	152 653	Against	9 805
Sth Aust.	For	65 990	Against	17 053
Tasmania	For	13 437	Against	791
Queensland	For	38 488	Against	30 996
Total	For	377,988	Against	141,386

Western Australia still refused to take part, but they did eventually get their referendum, albeit under questionable circumstances. Their referendum was held on July 31st, 1900, which was three weeks after Queen Victoria had assented to the Constitution Bill. Although the Western Australian vote was in favour of federation, fortyfour thousand in favour, compared to nineteen thousand, six hundred and ninetyone against, the Bill which had been agreed to in London, did not include Western Australia as an "original colony".

The total final count, including Western Australia, was four hundred and twenty two thousand, seven hundred and eighty eight (422,788) for federation and one hundred and sixty one thousand, and seventy seven (161,077) against. Statistically, compared to the estimated population of all the colonies in 1899, this represented eleven percent in favour of federation. However, because of the restricted and qualified vote, and the exclusion of most of the women, if not all of them, coupled with the knowledge that voting was not compulsory, it is difficult to say just what percentage of the then population did approve federation. Hence, the claim that the "Australian people" approved the draft Constitution is a quite untruthful statement for several reasons

- First, the male voters were only asked to approve, or reject, federation
- Very few voters ever had access to the draft document, and even if they did, most would not have been in a position to understand it.
- The British government demanded and got, amendments to the draft document before they were prepared to present it to Parliament, and subsequently, to the Queen for assent.
- As a result, the document passed by the British Parliament was not the document related to the federation referendums in Australia, and the 'Australian people' were never asked to approve this new document.
- On top of that, by excluding females from the referendum, as well as an unidentified number of males, the final numbers of assenting voters would fall well short of anything like majority approval.
- And lastly, the people generally, and certainly the sizeable opposition to Federation, had virtually no say in the creation of the document.

We have now arrived at the point where the colonies of Australia have been given permission by the British government to join together in creating a larger federated colony of Britain, a colony to be called the Commonwealth of Australia.

In fact, that was the original title of the Bill which was passed through the British Parliament on the ninth of July 1900 - *"The British Colony of the Commonwealth of Australia Constitution Act 1900 (UK)"*.

It is this very same Bill which Australia uses today as their primary law for the government, the courts, and the people.

In the next lesson, we will investigate how the Federal Government was set up and how it proceeded to operate.

LESSON 5

Having now determined that our "piece of paper" is actually the Constitution of Australia, we need to have a copy of this document in front of us as we continue our investigation.

The first government

Now that the British government had given their enlarged colony of Australia a Constitution, which was essentially a contractual arrangement setting up a system for all the separate colonies to work together; it was time to put the arrangement in place. From our research, the uniqueness of this situation never seems to be emphasised, or even recognised. How does one go about setting up a central government when there is nothing to start with, no elected members, no bureaucracy, no place to work from, simply a "piece of paper" saying it can exist? And what does this "piece of paper" say about the sort of government it will allow to govern the Australian colonies?

Our detective work is now at the stage where we need to call in the 'forensic experts' to closely examine all the available physical evidence.

That physical evidence is a copy of the "piece of paper" we have been investigating. It is now available as the Constitution of the Commonwealth of Australia, and printed by the Commonwealth Information Service. (It's also available on the internet)

A forensic examination of the "evidence"

Because the newly formed colony of Australia needs to set up a government, our first step is to see what sort of government is described in the Constitution.

Obviously, we start at the beginning of the booklet in front of us, and to our surprise we find no reference to the correct and proper title for the British Act of their Parliament.

This in itself appears unusual because, it is the British government that actually owns this "piece of paper", and not the Australian government, and far less the Australian people.

Once we overcome our surprise, we find the Index starts by listing nine "Covering Clauses" of the Act. And there, at number nine, is a clause entitled "Constitution".

What's going on here?

The cover of the booklet says, "The Constitution of the Commonwealth of Australia", and the heading of the index page say, "The Constitution", but we find that "The Constitution" is only one part of a nine part Act of the British Parliament.

There seems to be something wrong here, either the printers of this "piece of paper" have been given the wrong information, or somebody doesn't understand the history, but whichever it is, it is creating a false impression by ignoring the facts. One of the facts we should establish is who actually wrote these "covering clauses" and what are they supposed to represent? Are they to be read as an integral part of the "Constitution", or are they something outside of the "Constitution"?

When we read the actual clauses it becomes obvious they were written by the British government, and were not part of the draft Constitution compiled in Australia.

After the list of the "covering clauses" the Index follows on with "Chapter 1" – The Parliament. From a quick browse of the Index we see that there are eight Chapters covering one hundred and twentyeight Sections. This is all very intriguing, and it's going to require a much deeper examination to find out what's going on.

The "Covering Clauses"

When we open the booklet to the pages following the index we come to the actual start of the British Parliament's Act, but there is no clear reference to this fact. Instead, the page is again headed "The Constitution" and this is followed by some meaningless information in brackets – e.g. – (63 & 64 Victoria. Chapter 12)

This is followed by – "An Act to constitute the Commonwealth of Australia", and again in brackets (9th July 1900)

From our earlier investigation, we can interpret the word "Victoria" as referring to Queen Victoria of England, and not the State of Victoria in Australia. We also recognise that the date refers to the date on which this Act was passed in the British Parliament.

Why is there an apparent attempt to hide the truth in relation to this document?

The nine "covering clauses" are then listed under a few brief opening sentences. In most circumstances, these opening sentences would be described as a "preamble", a statement explaining the purpose and intent of the document.

Opening Statements

Opening statements come in several forms. Some books have a "Foreword", which describes aspects of the book and the author's intentions, or background. Technical papers often start with an "Abstract" that briefly covers the content of the article. Some Constitutions start off with a Preamble, which briefly expounds the philosophical intent and purpose of the document. Whether the Constitution is for an organisation, a community group, or a nation of people, the principles of the Preamble need to be taken into account when applying the Constitution.

Any such Preamble must always be an integral part of a Constitution, as it sets the tone and standards that have to be observed in administration, or in the case of a government, its responsibility to act honourably on behalf of the people. In modern day parlance, a Preamble is akin to a "Mission Statement", which defines the purpose and aims of an organisation – and governments are about the biggest organisations in any country.

The Preamble of the British Act of Parliament

As we noted above, this Preamble, and the clauses, were written by the British government with the express intention of including them as part of the Act.

Actually, these opening sentences are very important in defining the intent and purpose of the Act, although there could be some questions about parts of the meaning.

The preamble commences:

"Whereas the people of New South Wales, Victoria, South Australia, Queensland and Tasmania .... have agreed ......"
You will probably notice that Western Australia is not included, but that is explained in lesson three, when a referendum was held after the Act had already been passed by the British Parliament and signed by Queen Victoria.

The "agreement" to unite as a federated colony is correct, but there is a question about the acceptance of the draft Constitution which was altered by the British government. It is not the same draft that was linked to the referendums in Australia. Although those referendums only asked the eligible people if they agreed to federate the colonies, the acceptance of the draft Constitution was implied, or assumed. It was also a draft Constitution which most of the voters had never seen.

That altered document, which is now the "evidence' we are examining, has never been put to the Australian people for their acceptance – no one in Australia had the opportunity to review the alterations, and no one, apart from the five people who took the draft to London, were ever asked if they agreed with the changes. And did these five people have a choice anyway?

Another interesting anomaly

Semantics can be an absorbing study for some people, as it deals with the way words are used, and particularly in their historical and cultural context. Our interesting anomaly deals with the word "Whereas", which is the first word of this legal Act of the British Parliament.

"Whereas the people..." has a totally different meaning to the words used in the Constitution of the United States of America – that Constitution starts with the words "We, the people...."

"We, the people..." clearly and precisely defines "the people" as the owners, and originators, of the American Constitution.

In the case of the British Act creating the Australian Constitution, *"Whereas the people..."* simply confirms that "the people" had (supposedly) agreed to something they were offered. It does not proclaim ownership, it does not identify "the people" as the creators, but it does portray them in the role they are expected to play, then and now, in accepting (or rejecting if given the chance) what is presented to them. This was the policy and attitude behind the referendums of 1898, 1899 and 1900, and it has remained the same for every referendum in Australia since that time.

That attitude is another issue we shall have to look at in a later lesson.

The other significant thing about this anomaly is the fostered belief that the meanings of "Whereas the people…" and "We the people…." are the same, when clearly they are not. The Australian Constitution was never written for or by "the people' – it was written for and by the politicians and lawyers, with the intent of making it a document to maintain the system they were used to, and to preserve the status quo of that day and age. In this respect, it has been very successful!

Defining Australia's status

If we assume that everything written in our "piece of paper" has been written for a purpose, and it is not just random scribbling to fill up space, we must therefore examine the purpose of the words.

What are "the people' supposed to have agreed to?

According to the rest of the opening sentence, they have agreed to –*"unite in one indissoluble Federal Commonwealth under the crown of the United Kingdom of Great Britain and Ireland ……"*

Does semantics play another part in the remainder of that first sentence? For example, how are we to interpret the word, "indissoluble"? Does it really mean the normal and correctly understood interpretation? And how does anyone guarantee that an agreement between people can be made "indissoluble"? Were it possible to do so, this injunction would prevent any government from changing Australia's status at any time in the future. And how would such a condition be enforced?

If this legal document is to be maintained, it means that Australia will remain under the British crown *"forever"* – it means the Australian people will *always* be classed as British subjects, as long as this document remains in force.

That last bit, **"as long as this document remains in force"** is fairly important as far as Australia is concerned. Because this Act is an Act of the British Parliament, and like all legislation coming out of any Parliament, it can be cancelled, repealed, or "rescinded" as is another legal word. It means that technically, only the British Parliament has the legal "power," and legal ability, to change Australia's status from a colony to a free and independent nation.

The British government could actually do this at any time they wished, and they could do it with or without the approval of the Australian people, the Australian politicians, or the Australian lawyers. The British Parliament can rescind the Act anytime they choose, and this is something that should have been done back in 1920 when Australia was admitted as a member of the League of Nations.

While many people in Australia harbour the wrong impression that Australia is an independent nation, the idea of independence is a rather complicated, unfinished and unsatisfactory story, which we will also deal with in a later lesson.

Independence is also a concept that was never a part of the Constitution, as is confirmed by Sir Henry Parkes, '*Federation is not independence. It is a chance for the colonies more effectively to unite with the Mother country in forming an Empire such as has never yet been formed*'.

The Queens' permission

The last sentence of the preamble clearly confirms the status of the British monarchy, which as we discovered earlier, exists with the consent of the British Parliament, and the 1701 Act of Settlement.

The sentence states that the Queen is allowed to approve this Act because, she has been given the "advice" and permission "of the Lords Spiritual and Temporal and Commons" to do so.

While it might be interesting to discover the exact definition of "the Lords Spiritual and Temporal", essentially it means the House of Lords in the UK Parliament. The "Commons" means the lower House of Commons, consisting of the "ordinary' people outside of the aristocracy. Britain still retains the remnants of the feudal system, and remains a very class conscious nation, which is why many of the population still think of themselves as "subjects" of the Queen.

The other clauses

Having dealt with the "preamble", if we might be so bold as to refer to the three opening sentences as such, we can now look at the clauses.

Clause 1 allows a short title to be used, which explains why that title is used on our "evidence" document.

Clause 2 says the provisions of the Act are to be passed onto the Queen's heirs and successors, which is a necessary condition to maintain the "indissoluble" stipulation of the "preamble".

Clause 3 makes a provision to include Western Australia, if the people so agree and it also stipulates that the Act must be proclaimed within a year of it passing though the British Parliament. The clause also provides for the Queen to appoint a Governor General to the newly formed Commonwealth, but only after the Act has been proclaimed. Our close investigation finds an interesting semantic question with the wording of this part of the clause. It says "But the Queen _may_ ...." as distinct from "But the Queen _shall_ ...".

Why is the Queen given an option to appoint a Governor General? What would happen if she decided not to appoint one? According to the current practice in Australia, it is essential that there is always a Governor General in place; so why use "may" when the obvious word should be "shall"? Is there a logical answer to this?

More confusion caused by the other clauses.

Clause 4 is a bit of open slather for the several colonies in that they are free to make laws between the time the Act is passed by the British parliament and before it officially comes into force at the date it is formally proclaimed. Presumably, this is to allow continuity of the colonial administration, but any law made in this period could be challenged if it were to be in conflict with future Commonwealth laws.

Clause 5 is a bit of a funny one. Suddenly, the "colonies" in Clause 4 are converted to "States". The clause also defines the extent of coverage for any laws made by the Commonwealth Parliament, which exempts British war ships, and applies conditions to other British ships.

Clause 6 is another funny one, as it seems to be making a law by converting the status of the colonies into that of "States," and it even throws New Zealand into the mix. The significance, or benefit of the status change, is not explained, and neither is a reason given for the change of status, let alone any details of what process is involved to changing a colony to a State.

Apart from allowing a shortened title of "Commonwealth" to be used for the name Commonwealth of Australia, the reason and purpose of this clause is confusing. It is also unclear why there is a need to refer to "the Original States" as if this implies some distinction between them and Western Australia.

Clause 7 is actually a proper legal process in repealing an unnecessary, and now redundant Act, but it does stipulate that any laws made under that Act shall remain in force until otherwise repealed. However, the last sentence of this clause does raise an unexplained side issue. It seems to imply that both colonies and States can exist within the Commonwealth, and each can have their own Parliaments. That seems ambiguous, but the sentence does give any of these Parliaments the authority to repeal the leftovers from the Federal Council Act they don't like.

Clause 8 Again, some of the wording of this clause is somewhat obscure. It is quite clear in stating the Colonial Boundaries Act 1895 shall not apply to any colony that "becomes a State", but the wording, "becomes a State" seems to contradict Clause 6 which implies the colonies are converted to "States". If Clause 8 is relevant, it implies there is a process which the colonies have to go through to become "States".

However, the one thing that is very clear is the final phrase, *"but the Commonwealth shall be taken to be a self-governing **COLONY** for the purposes of the Colonial Boundaries Act".*

This Clause 8 does confirm that the Commonwealth of Australia remains a colony of Britain. (And it remained so until its status is changed to that of a "Dominion" of Great Britain in 1907)

Clause 9 is quite clear and explicit in stating, *"The Constitution of the Commonwealth shall be as follows:-"*

The Clause then proceeds to set out the details of the "piece of paper" we started to investigate in lesson one. This clause proceeds to list the details of the Constitution, which now includes all the amendments demanded by the British government before it was presented in their Parliament.

Why do we need to investigate these clauses?

The reason we need to investigate these clauses is because of the confusion that surrounds them. There are various arguments about whether or not the eight preceding clauses should be taken into account when dealing with the actual Constitution. Some people say they should, and other say they shouldn't.

Although the Constitution doesn't have a "preamble", the question of whether the courts can ignore the eight preceding parts of the British Act is not clarified anywhere in Clause 9.

Can the clauses one to eight of the Act be separated from Clause 9, "The Constitution"?

Lay people continually misread *"Whereas the people..."* to mean the same as "We the people", and they thereby assume the first part of the Act is relevant to Clause 9, *"The Constitution".* The legal profession seem to say the opposite.

To find out what sort of government is described for the Commonwealth, we shall start investigating the details of Clause 9 in the next lessons.

LESSON 6

The actual Constitution

As we are now starting to get into the Constitution "proper", as distinct from the Act of the British Parliament, we will be investigating it from the point of view of an ordinary person. After all, it is the most important "piece of paper" in all our lives, and affects virtually everything we do. It is only right and proper that ordinary people should be able to read and understand what this "piece of paper' says, and we shouldn't need a law degree to do that.

So, we will examine this document in a rational and objective way, to see if what is written is the way the Constitution is applied in practice.

If people cannot read and understand what is written, then it clearly is not a Constitution written for the people, but I think we already know that.

Investigating the Constitution's form of government

As we said in the last lesson, the new federated colony, which the Constitution has allowed to be call the *"Commonwealth"*, is now at the stage where it needs to set up an entirely new central government. So, what does the Constitution say about the type of organisation that needs to be established?

Obviously, Chapter 1, entitled *"The Parliament"* has to be the first clue as to where we start.

Section 1 of Chapter 1 is quite clear;

"The legislative power of the Commonwealth shall be vested in a Federal Parliament, which shall consist of the Queen, a Senate, and a House of Representatives, and which is hereinafter called The Parliament, or The Parliament of the Commonwealth."

So; the Parliament consists of the Queen, a Senate and a House of Representatives.

The terms, Senate and House of Representatives, are taken from the US Constitution, and are used as a substitute for the English Parliament, which has its House of Commons and the House of Lords. The colonies had a Legislative Assembly, which equates to the House of Commons, and their Legislative Council was similar to the House of Lords. In the UK, the members are appointed to the House of Lords, but the colonies used both appointment and a restricted election system for their Legislative Councils.

The Governor General

Section 2 deals with the Governor General because, the Queen does not live in Australia. The section provides for the appointment of a Governor General with some unidentified "powers" as the Queen may give him. In those days, the tradition was that Governor General always had to be a male, but this is not stated in the Constitution Act.

Section 3 makes the position of Governor General a very lucrative job because, it says the Australian government has to pay him ten thousand pounds each year he's in the position. This was an extremely high salary for the 1900's, and if we converted it to today's currency, it would be close to one and a half million dollars.

We could do the research to find out what salary is paid to the current Governor General, but we would be pretty certain in saying it isn't anything like the above amount. It seems fairly obvious that this salary was one of the conditions demanded by the British government, as it is not likely to be within the authority of the "founding fathers" in Australia. Bear in mind, that one hundred pounds a year would have been considered a good amount for a lot of the people in 1900, and many were on far less.

The Politician's loophole

Why are we so certain the Governor General isn't being paid one and a half million dollars today? Because; this is the first time in the Constitution where the politicians slipped in their little catch phrase, *"until parliament otherwise provides"*.

We will find this little phrase used repeatedly throughout the Constitution, and part of the evidence we could collect is to count the number of times it is used. This is probably the most important phrase in the whole of the Constitution because; it allows Parliament to alter the Constitution without having to get the permission of the people. Obviously, predicting the future has never been a particularly strong, or reliable, characteristic of the human race, and it seems to be a pronounced weakness with politicians. Hence, the "founding fathers" have introduced an element of flexibility into the Constitution through giving the Parliament the ability to make amendments, *"as they otherwise see fit"*. In the case of the Governor General's salary, that would be a reasonable and specific use for the loophole.

The problem arises when the loophole is used in non-specific ways, and has the effect of altering the original intent and meaning of the Constitution. It will be those cases we will have to examine more closely.

Section 4 says the Governor General is not allowed to receive any other pay while he's in the job, which is also fair enough, but the actual description of the job is a bit strange. It says the Governor General's duties are to *"administer the government"*, but it doesn't define what this means.

Section 5 does clarify this a little by saying it's up to his discretion to decide when Parliament can meet, but it also says he can close Parliament by issuing a Proclamation *"at his pleasure"*. However, it does slip in the words, *"or otherwise"*, but without explaining what other conditions might apply. The section also says he can dissolve the House of Representatives by a similar process of issuing a Proclamation, *"or otherwise"*. The meaning of those two words is not defined so, it is an open book as to how the Governor General can act.

This section makes the distinction between the Parliament and the House of Representatives, which as we noted in **Section 1** of Chapter I, the term "Parliament" must include the Senate and the Queen, as well as the House of Representatives. From this, does it mean the Governor General only has the authority under the Constitution to dissolve the House of Representatives, and not the Senate? The section goes on to say that the Governor General must summon the Parliament to sit within thirty days after any general election. That's fair enough.

When it comes to forming the Commonwealth Government for the first time, the Governor General must do this within 6 months from when the Act is proclaimed in Australia. That proclamation happened on the 1st January 1901.

Section 6 says that Parliament must meet at least once a year, but it does not limit how many other times the Governor General may see fit to call the Parliament into session. From the reading of the Constitution, it seems we have a very powerful position given to the Governor General. He has the power to open and close Parliament when he likes, he can dissolve the House of Representatives, presumably, if they do something he doesn't like, and he is responsible for *"administering"* the government. A bit later, in Section 68, we find the Governor General is also the Commander in Chief of the armed forces.

None of this wording in the Constitution seems to conform to the idea that Australia is a "democratic" colony; in fact, it sounds more like the Governor General has dictatorial powers that are backed by the military. There again, from our investigation into the earlier history in creating this "piece of paper", we did learn that "democracy" was never a part of the discussions, if anything, it was avoided and totally rejected by the "founding fathers".

Part II – The Senate

Now we come to the part that defines what is considered, "the Upper House" of the Parliament. The thinking here is based on the Legislative Councils from the colonies, or States as they are now called. Each of the Legislative Councils consisted of a smaller number of members than the Legislative Assemblies. The Council members were either appointed by the Governor, or were elected by their peers, who could only vote if they qualified in terms of property, wealth and graduate qualifications. Thus, the Legislative Council was the House of the rich and powerful in the colonies, and this is largely how the Senate was viewed, and why it is referred to as the "Upper House". We also know that the colonial members were not paid a salary during their term in office.

Section 7 simply says that each State shall be considered as a single electorate, and the people of each State shall elect six members to sit in the Senate. However, it makes one exception for Queensland by allowing the Queensland Parliament to divide the State into divisions and allocate the number of Senators to each division.

The Section further qualifies the arrangements for the Senate by saying that each State must have a minimum of six Senators, and that the members are elected for a period of six years.

Anomalies in Section 7 for applying the politician's loophole

If we look at this Section closely we see that it refers to the *"Original States"*, which must be the States listed in the opening paragraph of the Act, namely, New South Wales, Victoria, South Australia, Queensland and Tasmania. Does this imply that a non-original State, that is Western Australia, can be treated differently?

While the logical answer to that question would be "no", the poor wording of the section could allow the answer to be "yes". It is in this section that we again come across the phrase, *"until Parliament otherwise provides"*. In other words, this Constitution can be altered by Parliament without having to go to a referendum of the people.

That above phrase, or a variation of it, is used three time in this one section, and it is in the third paragraph where it could allow a "yes' answer to the question about Western Australia.

The paragraph says, *"Until the Parliament otherwise provides there shall be six senators for each Original State."* Hypothetically, the loophole truly does allow Parliament to treat Western Australia differently because; the wording can be read as saying the six Senators only applies to the Original States.

Obviously, the meaning and intent of the constitution is that every State, whether Original or not, must have a minimum of six Senators. Based on the wording of this section, Parliament could, if they so choose, treat Western Australia differently, and thereby alter the perceived intent of the Constitution. If that were to happen, it really should be an issue that must go to a referendum of the people. Neither Parliament nor the Governor General should be allowed to make such alterations by legislation, but altering the intent of the Constitution by legislation is a practice the politicians have used repeatedly.

Section 8 also provides another loophole for the politicians, by slipping the words, *"or by Parliament"*. This means that

Parliament can change the meaning and intent of the Constitution by making the qualifications for electors of the Senate different from those required for the House of Representatives. At least this section prohibits multiple voting, which had been the accepted practice in the colonies.

What could have been the motivation for including this loophole? Did the "founding fathers" harbour some hidden agenda to convert the Senate into the equivalent of the British House of Lords – a House for the aristocracy of the new Federation?

In terms of the current "democratic" thinking, something that didn't apply in 1900, it is entirely natural that the qualification for electors should be the same for both Houses of Parliament.

Section 9 While this Section would seem quite logical, the Constitution would have been immeasurably strengthened by setting out the guiding principles that had to be observed in making the laws for choosing Senate candidates. For example, Mr John Macrossan was apparently the only member of the 1891 Convention who correctly saw that the Senate would be dominated by political parties. In which case, the members would be compelled to represent their party rather than the State they were elected to represent. Would it not be prudent to prohibit the encroachment of political parties in the selection of candidates for the Senate? Could this be a principle worth considering?

Another possibility could be to require secret ballots for all decision making in the Senate, thus allowing the members to exercise their discretion in choosing which responsibility they deem the most important?

There are several other issues that could form an appropriate set of guiding principles without trying to spell out the details in this section.

Section 10 Wow – what a mish-mash of loopholes – *"Until the Parliament otherwise provides, but subject to this Constitution, the laws in force in each State, for the time being, relating to elections for the more numerous House of the Parliament of the State shall, as nearly as practicable, apply to elections of senators for the State."*

This seems to give the politicians open slather to determine how they want to rig the election for Senators.

Where are the limits for what the politicians are allowed to do? We already know that the colonial laws for elections to the two houses of the colonial Parliaments varied from colony to colony, even to allowing the Governor's appointment of members for the Legislative Councils. Does this section allow those practices to continue? Why would the "founding fathers" condone such 'sloppy' wording, unless they did so for a specific purpose?

We also come across another anomalous phrase in *"but subject to this Constitution"*, which seems to have no definitive meaning unless it is referenced to some particular sections.

Section 11 This Section is rather non-sensible because, it doesn't provide for how many States may not have representatives, or the reason why representatives might fail to be chosen. If there were challenges in five States and only one State were cleared to sit in the Senate, why should they be allowed to *"despatch business"* as usual?

This would be a very easy situation to clarify by defining a couple of basic guidelines for when the Senate can *"despatch business"*. The obvious solution is to specify a number of Senators necessary to make up a quorum before any *"business"* can be *"despatched"*. **Section 22** does set a quorum for the Senate at one third of *"the whole number of the Senators"*, but there are different ways to interpret the meaning of this phrase. It would have been much clearer to say a quorum is one third *"the total number of Senators allowed by this Constitution"*.

Section 12 Again we have that curious use of the word "may", *"The Governor of any State may cause writs to be issued….."* Why is the State Governor given an option to issue writs – what happens if he chooses not to do so?

Assessing our Investigation to date

Our investigation into the Constitution document seems to be taking us in a new direction. We are finding a number of inexplicable examples in the wording of the document. This is raising questions about the motivation, reason and intent behind what is written. It is fairly safe to say that the "founding fathers" were all well educated professionals, and all of them would have had a good command of the English language, so why are we finding so many unanswered questions about the way this document is written.

Even if we were to attribute this to the culture of the times, why should today's reader have to transport themselves back a hundred and ten years in order to understand what is meant?

Is this proof of the inappropriateness of the Constitution in terms of today? How can anyone interpret the intent of the document if the meaning of the words has changed over time?

As there are another eleven sections to deal with in this Chapter on the Senate, we shall deal with those in the next lesson.

LESSON 7

The Senate

A number of questions have been raised from our close examination of the first twelve sections of the Constitution. Those sections relate to the conditions for establishing the Senate, but the wording is not very clear. As we continue to examine the remaining eleven sections we shall see whether this pattern is maintained.

Section 13 deals with splitting the Senators into two "classes". This is to occur at the very first sitting of the House, and subsequently, at the first sitting after any dissolution of the House. Now this is curious because, we know from **Section 5** in Part 1 that the Governor General only has the authority to dissolve the House of Representatives, but there is no reference to him having the power to dissolve the Senate.

So, how does the Constitution provide for dissolving this "upper House"?

That's a question to which we need to find an answer. But what is the reason for splitting the House into two "classes"? And why describe them as "classes" – is this some sort of discriminatory distinction? It would seem logical to assume all the elected Senators would be considered equal; hence the term "group" would seem more appropriate than "class". Maybe, that is just a matter of semantics, but there again; class consciousness was very prevalent in the day and age of the nineteenth century.

The anomalous use of the phrase "as near as practical"

The section says the Senators must be divided into two "classes", *"as nearly equal in number as practical"*. Either the "founding fathers" were not very strong on mathematics, or they had anticipated that Western Australia would be treated differently, as we noted in **Section 7**. If each State had to have an equal number of Senators, and the minimum had to be six members, then there is no question of a division being *"as near as practical"*. However, this wording does throw another light on **Section 7**, which allows "Parliament" – meaning both Houses, to increase or reduce the number of Senators for each "original" State, provided the minimum is six Senators for each State. The implication of *"as near as practical"* is that each of the "original" States could have their number of Senators increased to an odd number, e.g., seven or nine.

What's the mechanism for arranging the split?

Without defining how the split should be made, or why, the Section then says that the office of the first "class" of the split shall become vacant at the expiration of (the third year) **three years**. (This wording in brackets was changed by Australia's first Referendum in 1906)

As the principle of the Senate is to provide equal representation for each of the "original" States, (**Section 7**) why isn't the method for arranging the split defined as slitting each of the State's representatives in half. That way, the balance between the States would be preserved – UNLESS – Parliament were to increase the number of Senators to an uneven number, then the *"as near as practical"* would apply.

Australia's first Referendum in 1906

For some reason, Prime Minister Deakin, saw some subtle difference between the original wording of "the third and sixth year" and held a referendum to amend the Constitution wording to **"three and six years"**. As Section 7 sets the term of office for the Senators at six years, *"the sixth year"*, was the year for expiration of office for the second "class" of Senators. The Referendum changed the wording to *six years."*

There were two other relatively minor changes made to this section as a result of the Referendum, and we will look at those separately. None of the changes appeared to represent any increase in the Commonwealth Government's power, and that seems to be the key for arranging a "successful" Referendum.

Why were these terms changed?

What is the significant difference in the change of the above terms?

Does "the sixth year", or "third year" mean that an election for the Senate can be held at any time **within** the nominated year? If that is the case, then changing the term to a definitive "six and three years" would seem to imply that the Senators must serve their full three or six years before an election can be held.

All this seems to reflect very poor consideration in drafting this Constitution document, especially when changes were deemed necessary just six years after the Act was proclaimed.

Did some complications arise with the first Commonwealth elections, which occurred in 1901 and 1904? If so, what were the complications and why did they initiate the change in wording? There has to be some significance in this to justify a nation wide Referendum?

The next change resulting from the Referendum of 1906

The next sentence of this **Section 13** reads, *"The election to fill vacant places shall be made* ~~in the year at the expiration of which~~ **within one year before** *the places are to become vacant".*

The amendment is highlighted and the words deleted are crossed out. Again, the significance of the change is unclear, as well as being confusing. The original wording, which was *"in the year at the expiration of which"* actually seems quite explicit and understandable. The election must occur at some time within the third or sixth year. From that we would assume the office would only change hands at the expiration of the full three, or six years of the term. On the other hand, the changed wording, *"within one year __before__"* seems to imply that the election has to occur at least twelve months before the term of office is to expire.

Why was this change deemed necessary?

I think we have a valid right to assume that things are done for a reason, but it is difficult to see the reasons for the changes under discussion.

The fourth change resulting from the 1906 Referendum.

There does seem to be some logic in this fourth change as the original wording set the Senator's terms of office as commencing, *"on the first day of January"* following the election. As the Act was proclaimed on the 1st of January 1901, and the first election had to be held within six months of that date, setting the date to take office meant that there was at least a six months gap before the first lot of Senators could sit in the Senate. In fact, the first Commonwealth elections were held on the 29th of March 1901, which meant the Senators were unable to sit until the 1st of January 1902, if we assume the Constitution was correctly followed.

The amendment changed the date from *"the first day of January"* to the *"first day of July"*, but that would only come into effect in 1906. While this amendment was supposed to be an improvement, it only worked when elections were held in March or April. When the elections were held after July, which has been the case for two thirds of the elections up to 2013, the incoming Senators have to wait more than six months before they can take their seat.

Section 14 adds another phrase to the list that allows Parliament to make changes by including, *"make such provision .... as it deems necessary,"* although in this case, it does limit Parliament to, *"maintaining regularity in rotation"*. However, we still haven't discovered the reason, or the Constitutional authority for needing a rotational system.

The main thrust of this Section relates to an increase, or a decrease in the number of Senators allowed for each State. Our research has found that the number of Senators per State was increased to ten in 1950. In 1975, the Territories of Canberra and Northern Territory were each allowed two Senators, and in 1985, the number of State Senators was increased to twelve. Thus, as of today, the Senate consists of seventysix Senators.

How do Territory Senators fit in?

The Territory Senators were added under **Section 122** of the Constitution which allows the Commonwealth Government to make laws for the Territories, including allowing them representation in either Houses of Parliament under *"terms which it thinks fit"*.

Section 15 Casual Vacancies

Section 15 made provision for replacing a State Senator, if and when a vacancy occurred. This could happen if a Senator died, became incapacitated, and was expelled or resigned.

Section 15 was the focus of the 1977 Referendum when the voters were asked a simple question, *"It is proposed to alter the Constitution to ensure as far as practicable that a casual vacancy in the Senate is filled by a person of the same political party as the Senator chosen by the people and for the balance of his term. Do you approve the proposed law?"*

The voters were offered no explanations as to the ramifications of a "Yes" result.

This is a classic example of how the Government manipulates the Referendums. They ask a simple question, and then proceed to insert quite profound alterations to the wording. In this case they replaced the original two hundred and four words of the Section with one thousand and fortyeight words as a result of the "Yes" vote.

The ramification was the introduction of "political parties" into the Constitution, something the founders deliberately chose to ignore, even though the influence of political parties was well known back in 1890. **This amendment represents a fundamental change in the concept for creating the Senate. The Senate was supposed to be a State's House, where the Senators were elected to represent their State. By changing Section 15 in this way, it clearly confirms that representation of the political party takes precedent over representing the State.**

The sole purpose of this amendment was to eliminate the risk of the ruling political party losing the balance of power in the Senate.

Under the original wording of this section, the State Governor had the power to choose any person whom he considered best suited for representing the State, but the Westminster system transfers that authority to the State Premier. While these casual vacancy appointments only apply to the remaining term of office until the next election, they could still impact on the Federal government if the State government were held by the opposition party.

The "sinister" bit in amending Section 15

What is a bit sinister about this amendment is the fact it was written well before the results of the Referendum was decided. This is proven by the last paragraph, which commences, *"If, at or before the commencement of the Constitution Alteration (Senate Casual Vacancies) 1977, a law to alter the Constitution entitled "Constitution Alteration (Simultaneous Elections) 1977" came into operation,....".*

There were four questions asked in the 1977 Referendum, and the second question was, *"It is proposed to alter the Constitution to ensure that Senate elections are held at the same time as House of Representatives elections.*

Do you approve the proposed law?"

It so happened that this question was answered with a "No", which meant the people did not approve of the idea for having simultaneous elections of both Houses of Parliament.

The question is was the full text of the proposed amendment to **Section 15** ever made public before the referendum? Were the ramifications of changing the principle concept of the Senate from a State's House to a political party House, ever clearly explained? Obviously, the Government knew they were in direst contravention to the intention of the founders, when they surreptitiously wrote "political parties" into the Constitution. The Government also contravened Section 128 of the Constitution by not presenting *"the proposed law"* at the time of the referendum. **There is no provision in the Constitution for any referendum to be held on the basis of a simplified question. Section 128 emphatically, and repeatedly, says** *"the proposed law"* **must always be presented to the people.**

Is it any wonder why the people do not trust the Government when they come up with proposals to change the Constitution?

The other Questions in the 1977 Referendum

In reference to the third and fourth questions asked at this Referendum, one dealt with altering the Constitution in respect to the retiring age of Federal Court Judges. As this did not seem to represent an increase in the Federal Government's powers, the question received a "Yes" vote. We will look at the ramifications of this question in a later lesson – a lesson dealing with the Judiciary

A similar "Yes" result was obtained with the fourth question, which was. *"It is proposed to alter the Constitution so as to allow electors in the territories, as well as electors in the states, to vote at referendums on proposed laws to alter the Constitution.*

Do you approve the proposed law?

At the time, this was not seen as an increase in the Government's powers, and the result was put into effect by twice adding two words to Chapter VIII, Alteration of the Constitution, **Section 128**, plus a short sentence referring to **Section 122** that dealt with Territories. The two words were, *"and Territories"*, and the sentence was, *"In this section, Territory means any territory referred to in section one hundred and twenty-two of this Constitution in respect of which there is in force a law allowing its representation in the House of Representatives".*

As this is a rather long lesson, we shall continue looking at the Senate in the next lesson.

LESSON 7A

Continuing with the Senate

In view of the various anomalies we have found in the previous fifteen sections of this Part II of Chapter 1, it seems advisable we should continue the same careful examination of the remaining eight sections.

Section 16 relates to the qualifications of a Senator, but instead of defining directly what these are, the section invites the reader to leap ahead because, it says the qualifications, *"shall be the same as those of a member of the House of Representatives."*

As the Constitution first deals with the Senate, the logical sequence should be to define the qualifications of the Senators, and then stipulate that the same qualifications must apply to members of the House of Representatives. If we assume that nothing is written in a Constitution without a reason, what could be a reason for reversing the natural sequence in defining the qualifications? Is it because the "founders" understood, and accepted the superiority of the House of Representatives over the Senate? If that is the case, why does the Constitution start with the Senate rather than the House of Representatives?

When these sorts of questions are raised, it must make an ordinary person wonder what went on in the minds of the "founders". Is the Constitution a document that was never intended to be read and understood by ordinary people?

From our investigation to date, that would certainly appear to be the case.

To move on to **Section 17.** Like the term Senate, this Section has its roots in the US Constitution because, it introduces the requirement for the Senators to "choose" one of their members to act as the Leader of the Senate. This position is given the title of, "President of the Senate".

What the section doesn't do is explain the process for "choosing" this "President" other than to say he can be "chosen", and dismissed, by a vote of the Senators. The "President" can also resign by writing a letter of resignation addressed to the Governor General.

One must assume that the leader of one of the two Houses of Parliament must be a reasonably important position. This would imply that the method of selecting a candidate, and the duties related to this office, should warrant, at least, some guidelines for definition in a Constitution.

Both these issues are completely ignored in the document we have before us.

As **Section 15** has introduced political parties into the Senate, is it right that a party with a majority can impose their views in selecting, and appointing a "President"?

Shouldn't the people have a say in how they would like to have the leader of this "upper" House selected and appointed?

Section 18 says the Senators can "choose" a replacement "President" to *"perform the duties"* if the elected one is absent, but again, there is no description of the duties related to this office, nor any details of the selection or "choosing" process for candidates. Hence, the same questions arise as in **Section 17.**

Section 19 provides for a Senator to resign by writing a letter to the "President", or if the President is not available, a letter to the Governor General. However, the wording is a bit confusing in respect to **Section 17.** That section specifically stipulates that the first business at the first sitting of a new Senate after an election is to "choose" a "President". This **Section 19** provides for a situation, *"if there is no President"*, which shouldn't occur if **Sections 17** and **18** are applied.

Is this another case of "sloppy" wording, or is there some unexplained situation where the Senate can operate without a "President"? On the other hand, are the "founders" trying to cover all foreseeable situations in this instance?

The "founders" normal procedure for covering all bases is to use the phrase, *"until Parliament otherwise provides,"* or words to that effect, but they didn't do so in this instance.

Section 20 is another one that is made difficult to understand, in part because of the lack of definitions for the terms used in the Constitution.

The wording of the Section is, *"The place of a senator shall become vacant if for two consecutive months of any session of the Parliament he, without the permission of the Senate, fails to attend the Senate."*

The confusion lies in the definition of the word, *"session"* – does this mean that a "session" lasts for two months or more, and the Senator has to miss a whole two months of sittings without permission before he's sacked?

Or does this mean that if he's absent for two consecutive months without permission, and doesn't attend any sessions of the Senate in that time, then there is grounds for dismissal? If the Senator were to attend only one day of a "session" in any two months, then this provision wouldn't apply. In other words, a Senator need only attend six days of sessions in any twelve months to circumvent getting permission to be absent.

Alternatively, does *"session"* refer to the whole term of office for which a Senator is elected? Another option is whether it refers to any twelve month period?

And why are the "sessions" related to "Parliament" rather than the Senate? From our earlier investigation it appeared that "Parliament" refers to both the Houses of Parliament. The wording really doesn't make sense. A further anomaly arises from the words, *"without the permission of the Senate"*. How does *"the Senate"* give its permission? Why isn't it a duty of the "President" to give permission, as distinct from the implication that all the other members of the Senate must be involved?

Section 21 Again, there is the inference that the Senate can function without having a President, but otherwise, the section sets out a procedure for notifying the relevant State Governor that a Senate vacancy has occurred. Apart from including, what should be the unnecessary words, *"or if there is no President"*, this section is understandable.

Section 22 The section deals with a Quorum that must apply for any session of the Senate. Actually, this section sets an extremely low attendance for establishing a quorum, which by any rational measure should be a minimum of at least fifty percent, plus one, of the total membership. Better still; the quorum should be set at two thirds the total number of Senators. Another anomaly arises with this section, as it creates a quite unnecessary complication. The actual wording reads, *"Until the Parliament otherwise provides, the presence of at least one-third of the whole number of the senators shall be necessary to constitute a meeting of the Senate for the exercise of its powers"*.

The problem comes about from the opening phrase, *"Until the Parliament otherwise provides..."*. Why is "Parliament" involved? Surely, this is a matter for the Senate to decide, and it shouldn't need to involve the House of Representatives?

And what happens if the "Lower" House tries to impose their wishes on the "Upper" House, and the Senate rejects the proposal?

By using the word "Parliament", it signifies that both Houses must agree to any change.

On the other hand, specifying a quorum to legitimise the *"exercise of its powers"* is a very important issue that shouldn't be available to either the "Parliament", or the Senate, to manipulate for the benefit of the politicians.

Most certainly, there should be a prohibition on reducing the numbers for a quorum below one third. By rights, the setting of a quorum should be a privilege of the people to decide, and not something that can safely be left in the hands of the "political party" that happens to be in power at any given time.

Section 23 Of all the twentythree sections in this Part II of the Constitution, this is the only one that is properly written and does not cause confusion. The wording is straight forward and unambiguous, and raises no questions as to its interpretation.

"Questions arising in the Senate shall be determined by a majority of votes, and each senator shall have one vote. The President shall in all cases be entitled to a vote; and when the votes are equal the question shall pass in the negative".

An Interesting Exercise

Having now made a detailed study of this Part II of the Constitution, it would be interesting exercises to have the students write their own versions of each of the sections.

They should write it in a way that it can be clearly understood by any citizen of Australia, and most importantly, the reader shouldn't need legal training to make sense of the content.

The students should be free to add additional sections if they feel this is necessary to make the process properly understood.

LESSON 8

Australia is NOT an Independent Sovereign Nation

If the Judges on the High Court of Australia are supposed to be the best legal brains in Australia, then they must have knowingly made a wrong decision in the Sue v Hill case of 1999. They declared the UK to be a foreign country and this is patently ludicrous, as we still use the law of the UK as our Constitution.

As an independent sovereign Nation, Australia has the **legal obligation to sever all political and Constitutional ties with Britain.** To do this they are required to have the British Act repealed, and to write their own Australian Constitution for adoption at a nation wide referendum of the Australian people.

It is an indisputable historical fact that Australia could have become an independent nation when we were invited to be signatories at the Treaty of Versailles on the 28th of June 1919.

It was then up to the Prime Minister, Billie Hughes, to take the proper legal steps in severing all the political and legal ties with Britain.

As it turns out, Billy Hughes has been the only Australia Prime Minister in the past ninetyfour years to attempt to do the right and proper thing to make Australia a sovereign and independent nation.

That necessary step was attempted by Prime Minister Hughes and his then Deputy, Earl Page, when they introduced a Constitution Bill to the Australian Parliament in 1921. In the face of a hostile reaction, they had to withdraw the Bill in December of that year.

The reaction to such a Bill is understandable in respect to the reality of the times. Australia had just come out of a horrendous war on behalf of the "mother country", and the sentiment was that Australia was part of Britain. Severing Australia's political ties with Britain was simply inconceivable.

Given the day and age in which the really monumental events of 1919 occurred, and even though they occurred virtually by accident, the philosophic foundations of the political thought at that time, precluded the possibility of drafting a new Constitution. Such an action proved beyond the conception and political reality of the day. The mentality of the times would never have been able to stretch to divorcing our ties with the 'mother country'. Consequently, future generations are left to sort out the mess.

The early quest for Independence

As far back as 1850, there have been people in Australia advocating independence along Republican lines, but it had never been particularly popular or well organised. The idea burst into flower in the latter part of the nineteenth century and produced some notable examples, not the least being Henry Lawson's journal, 'The Republican'. A number of other journals followed between 1887 and 1890, only to flounder in the face of the emerging push for federation.

The "unknown" phenomena arising from the First World War

While this phenomena is virtually unknown by the general public, many in the legal profession are completely aware of the events, but they have deliberately chosen to withhold the facts from the public.

An Imperial War Conference was held in London during 1917 to discuss the aftermath of "the war to end all wars". The plan was to set up an international organisation of the victorious nations involved in the war. The purpose of the organisation was to solve future disputes through mediation and diplomacy. This was the reason for creating the League of Nations. At these preliminary talks, Britain agreed with the support of Woodrow Wilson, the President of the United States, that Prime Minister Hughes and his Deputy, Sir Joseph Cook, should sign the League of Nations Treaty on behalf of Australia. This was in recognition of Australia's contribution to the war effort.

Conditions of Membership to the League of Nations

The League of Nations was an organisation made up of twentynine (supposedly) sovereign and independent countries, and their membership rules, Article XVIII and XX in their Covenant, stipulated that no member nation was allowed to use the laws of another member nation. As long as Australia continued to use the law of Britain as their Constitution, Australia was in breach of the rules for membership.

There is reputed to be a British government document that authorised the Dominion delegates to be appointed as representing fully independent nations, but the document was said to be classified as "secret" with a thirty year non-disclosure attachment. If this document does exist, it now seems impossible to locate its whereabouts.

Signatories to the Treaty

The League of Nations Treaty was signed on June 28th 1919, at Versailles in France, and Australia, **theoretically**, took its place in the world as an independent Nation. On September 10th

1919, Billie Hughes addressed the Commonwealth Parliament declaring, 'Australia has now entered into a family of nations on a footing of equality. Australia has been born in a blood sacrifice.'

This speech was delivered in the course of ratifying the Treaty of Versailles in the Commonwealth Parliament.

On January 10th 1920, the League of Nations became part of International Law, with Article X of the Covenant of the League of Nations guaranteeing the sovereignty of each of its twentynine members.

The aftermath of this event

It is clear that the Australian people did not understand the true impact of these events at the time, or since, but most Australian Parliaments since that date, did recognise there was an anomaly in defining Australia's status. Hence the 1942 Westminster Act and the 1986 Australia Act. It is somewhat inconceivable that the Judges of the High Court of Australia were not aware of the events of 1919 and 1920, but in 1999 we are led to believe that was the case.

A name change

In 1850, the British defined their settlements in Australia as Colonies, and in 1901, Britain granted the unification of these colonies into the Commonwealth of Australia. In 1907, the British Parliament changed Australia's status to that of 'the British Dominion of the Commonwealth of Australia', along with Canada, New Zealand and South Africa. At an Imperial Conference in 1911, a discussion took place about allowing the Dominions to have a say in treaties that involved them. Sir Wilfred Laurier asserted that "giving the Dominions the right to assent to a treaty was not an argument for separation", and Mr. Andrew Fisher, the then Prime Minister of Australia, agreed.

Proof of Australia's subservience to Britain

The unquestionable proof of our continued subservient status to Britain existed through to 1914. It comes from the fact that King George V declared war on behalf of the British Dominions of the Empire, and that included Australia.

Although Australia was under no direct threat as a result of the war in Europe, being British subjects, it was natural we would heed the call of the "mother country", and rush to her defence.

What does independence really mean?

Independence involves severing the legal Constitutional ties with England, as distinct from having the separate colonies come together as a federation. As we noted earlier, Sir Henry Parkes made that very clear when he said, *"Federation is not independence. It is a chance for the colonies more effectively to unite with the Mother country in forming an Empire such as has never yet been formed"*.

As the Constitution Act is a British Act owned by Britain, only their Parliament has the power to make changes, and ultimately, to repeal the Act. If Australia wants to make changes outside of the thirtynine provisions that allow the Australian Parliament to alter things by legislation, the Government has to call a referendum in Australia. If the referendum is successful, the Government can them send the changes to Britain for their approval.

In spite of the obvious legal ramifications for creating an independent Australia, many people today believe Australia is independent, and quite incredibly, that even includes Judges on the High Court of Australia who are supposed to know the law.

The Westminster Act

The first farcical attempt to try and formalise Australia's 'independence' from Britain was the Statute of Westminster, drawn up in 1931. This was a result of various resolutions passed by Imperial Conferences in 1926 and 1930, and because it was a statute that had to be passed by the British Parliament, it is further proof that Australia remained under the auspices of Britain. Legally, the Statute of Westminster was an 'international arrangement' involving Australia, Canada, South Africa and New Zealand, and under Article XVIII of the League of Nations Covenant, it had to be registered with them to become valid.

This was never done for obvious reasons!

The Australian government eventually adopted specific parts of this Statute in 1942, but the fact that the Statute itself was never registered with the League, meant that the Adoption Act, as passed by the Commonwealth Parliament, was also invalid in law. The Adoption Act itself is further flawed by virtue of its reliance on Royal Assent by the King of England who, in terms of Article XVIII of the League of Nations Covenant, represented a foreign power. Hypocritically, Britain conceded it no longer had any jurisdiction over the, supposedly, sovereign and independent Commonwealth of Australia, but still required legislation to be approved by the Monarch's representative in Australia.

The 1986 Australia Act

In June 1982, Malcolm Fraser began discussions with the State Premiers on ways to overcome, what was still recognised, as an anomalous relationship with the UK. Discussion continued under the new Prime Minister, Bob Hawke until June 1984. The outcome was another agreement to radically alter the Australian Constitution by creating the Australia Act of 1986.

The Australia Act was an attempt to try and make Australia appear independent. Unfortunately for the politicians, that Act had to be approved by the British Parliament before it could apply. Why an independent country needs the approval of another country for its laws to become valid, is a question that didn't seem to cross the minds of our political leaders. That is, apart from Justice Kirby who remarked, '*I know this is an eccentric and personal view, but I have always wondered what the UK Parliament was doing enacting law in 1986 in relation to Australia.*' This last comment confirms that the application of reason and logic, as applied to legal argument, is considered an 'eccentric' approach.

The major problem with the Australia Act was its attempt to make major alterations to the British Constitution Act. It really shouldn't have been passed by the British Parliament until it was agreed to by the people in Australia at a referendum.

How can Australia become a proper independent nation?

As we found in **Lesson 4**, only the British Parliament has the legal "power" to make Australia an independent nation, and they could do that simply by rescinding their Act for creating the Constitution of their federated colonies.

That would be the easiest and simplest way for Australia to be legally recognised as an independent nation. The Australian people would then have to write their own Australian Constitution without any ties to Britain and the Monarchy.

Of course, the Australian people could declare their independence themselves, if they so choose, but they could only do it by rejecting the current legal system we live under. In other words, they would have to follow the American example and have a revolution. It wouldn't have to be a war like revolution, if the Government of the day were to handle it properly and accept the will of the people.

However, virtually every Government tends to oppose any changes to the existing system, whatever changes are involved, and anyone who tries to make a change, immediately becomes a rebel, a traitor, a terrorist, or an extremist. Depending on which side of the fence one sits, if the people advocating change are supported by another country, they would be seen as "freedom fighters" by that country.

An interesting hypothetical situation

If the Australian people were to take unilateral action in declaring Australia an independent nation, it would create an interesting hypothetical situation.

Who would object if the majority of Australians wanted to go down that path?

Would Britain object? Probably not, as the Queen has already said she will accept any decision of the Australians if they want to change their head of State. If Britain were to object, they have the Governor General in their pocket, who under the Constitution, also happens to be the Commander in Chief of the Armed Forces. But is he "in their pocket"? Under the Westminster system, the Governor General is supposed to only act on the "advice" of the Prime Minister, but that's not a guaranteed thing, as Sir John Kerr demonstrated. This then introduces the reaction of the Armed Forces. Would they be prepared to obey the command of either the Governor General or the Prime Minister if ordered to stop a movement for independence?

And lastly, but not least, how would a successful independent movement proceed to take over the country?

Definitely an interesting hypothetical situation!

The perception and the reality

The First World War is portrayed as a catalyst that led to a virtual organic transformation of Australia from its Colonial/ Dominion status to that of a supposedly independent nation. This opportunity came about without any concerted effort or initiative from the general public. In fact, right up to this day, the public are generally unaware that any possible transformation could have taken place, let alone when and how it might have occurred. They are not alone in this field, as this same supposed lack of knowledge and understanding, applies to most politicians, and virtually all the legal fraternity, right through to the High Court of Australia. There certainly is a core of leading politicians and lawyers who are fully aware of how Australians have been deceived over the years. The 1986 Australia Act is clear proof of the deception that has been perpetuated for decades.

The invitation to join the League of Nations as a founding member in 1919 should have been the vehicle that changed our status from a Dominion of Britain to the independent nation we were supposed to be.

Unfortunately, it is at this point in our history, when all the 'great' minds of our 'supposedly' infallible legal fraternity, combined with the ignorance of the politicians of the day, failed to legally formalise our new status. Not only did the politicians omit formalising our independence from Britain, they also conveniently, or ignorantly, omitted to inform the general public of Australia that they were now, supposed to be, officially independent.

Recognition of the change status

That Australia's status, vis a' vis Britain, had changed was recognised, up to a point, by the next Prime Minister, Stanley Bruce. In 1923, he told the British Government, '*We have to try to ensure there shall be an Empire foreign policy which, if we are to be in any way responsible for it, must be one to which we agree and have assented. If we are to take any responsibility for the Empire's foreign policy, there must be a better system, so that we may be consulted and have a better opportunity to express the views of the people of this country. We cannot blindly submit to any policy which may involve us in war.*'

Again, it appears obvious that neither Bruce or his Government, nor anyone else in the Commonwealth Parliament, had any intention of carrying out what was required to cement the true significance of Australia's altered status.

Independence at that time in history was never a publicly oriented goal, nor was it an issue motivated by public or political sentiment, just as it was never the underlying purpose of membership with the League of Nations. In a technical sense, Australia gained her pseudo independence as a sovereign nation by default. Very few people at that time, or now, recognised the real significance of this event, or have since had the initiative to take the proper legal action required to certify this independence.

> The fact that it was not recognised for what it truly was, and the fact that it was never properly and legally formalised, in no way detracts from the reality that it did happen and we could have become an independent and sovereign nation, effective from June 28th 1919.

The late Professor G. Clements, Eminent UK QC and emeritus Professor in Law at Cambridge University, clearly understood the true legal position of the Australian Constitution when he remarked,

'The continued usage of the Australian Constitution Act (UK) by the Australian Governments and the judiciary is a confidence trick of monstrous proportions played upon the Australian people with the intent of maintaining power. It remains an Act of the United Kingdom. After joining the League of Nations in 1919, Australia became a sovereign nation. It had no further legal power to use, alter or otherwise tamper with another nation's legislation. Authority over the Australian Constitution Act lies not with the Australian government nor with the Australian people, it rests solely with the UK. Only they have the authority to repeal this legislation ...'

For anyone interested in a more detailed discussion on Australia's lack of independence as a sovereign nation they might like to visit the webpage www.aussieindependence.com

LESSON 9

Chapter 1 Part III the House of Representatives

As we continue our investigation into the Constitution document we need to compare it with the reality of how the system of Government is applied in practice.

Most of us know that the House of Representatives is really the major House in the parliamentary system, even though it is not dealt with first in the Constitution. There are a number of reasons why the House of Representatives is considered the more important, not the least being; this is the House where all the initial proposals for revenue laws must originate. Another significant reason is that the Prime Minister is always a member of this House.

In some respects, the Senate has an equal standing to the House of Representatives through its ability to approve or reject proposals, or its authority to propose amendments. Although none of this is spelled out in the Part II of the Constitution, it is the way the Westminster system allows the Senate to function. The Senate is prohibited from initiating revenue proposal, but they can suggest amendments. As a political party tactic, the Senate can also withhold their approval of a money bill, thus denying the government access to funds for running the country. Of course, none of these "rules" are included in the Constitution as they come from the unwritten "conventions" associated with the Westminster system. If we had a logical and rational Constitution many of these "rules" and resultant tactics would be addressed. "Conventions" are an issue we will examine later when we look at the Westminster system in more detail.

First, let us see what the Constitution says about the House of Representatives.

Section 24

At first glance this section is quite straight forward in defining how many members will be allowed to sit in the House of Representatives. It says, *"as near as practical"* the number of members shall be twice the number allowed for the Senate. That part isn't a problem, but the bit that says the members, *"shall be directly chosen by the people"* avoids explaining how this might happen. Logically, there should be a reference to a section of the Constitution that defines how elections are to be conducted.

What does, *"directly chosen by the people"* mean?

On reviewing the Index of the Constitution, we find there is no section that deals specifically with elections. One would think this is quite an important issue for a democratic system, and an issue that would justify at least some guidelines in the Constitution. But as we discovered in our earlier lessons, democracy was never an overriding concern of the "founding fathers".

In terms of semantics, what does the word *"directly"* mean? In the past, with all the qualifying conditions placed on candidates, coupled to the fact most politicians were not paid, it is highly likely most elections were between two contestants. In that case, being directly elected would apply if more than fifty percent of the limited number of qualified voters selected one of the candidates. After Federation, there was an increased awareness with politics, with the result that many elections involved a multiple number of candidates. In that situation, there was less chance of one candidate receiving more than fifty percent of the total votes, and thereby being *"directly"* elected.

It seemed hardly fair to allow a candidate with less than fifty percent of the votes to be elected. Obviously in that case, the majority of the voters did not approve of that candidate. Hence, an alterative system was devised to incorporate a system of *"indirect"* votes to be counted. This is the system known as preferential voting, which is now common practice in most elections. Thus, the eventual "winner" in many elections is dependent of the distribution of *"indirectly"* allocated "preference" votes.

If that is the case, how is that construed as being *"directly"* elected by the people?

The conduct of elections can be an involved subject, which we will also discuss in a later lesson.

To return to **Section 24;** we find it also includes the now familiar, *"until Parliament otherwise provides"*, which allows Parliament to amend the ways the number of members for the House of Representatives is determined.

Subsection (i) of this Section tries to define how a "quota" is determined, but it uses terms that in themselves are not defined. The actual wording of the subsection is:

(i) a quota shall be ascertained by dividing the number of the people of the Commonwealth, as shown by the latest statistics of the Commonwealth, by twice the number of the senators;

How to define terms used in the Constitution

To start with, what is a "quota", but more intriguing, how do we define the word *"people"* as counted in the census? Bear in mind, in 1890, virtually no women would have been considered as eligible voters in Federal elections, along with quite a number of "unqualified" men. And the "founding fathers" made sure Aborigines would be excluded by adding **Section 127** to the

Constitution. That section specifically stated Aborigines would not be counted in the Census. And what about the thousands of Chinese and South Pacific labourers who were brought to Australia to work in the goldfields and sugar cane industry? Were they to be counted in the census?

Was this part of the "original intention" of the "founding fathers", to ensure the status quo was maintained by excluding these "undesirable" voters from future elections?

As we now have a few insights into the thinking of that day and age, and a recognition of the low opinion regarding "democracy", it is more than likely that is what they intended.

However, times change, and most Australians now have a broader acceptance of the concept of "democracy", although there certainly isn't one universal definition of what that term really means. So, today the term *"people"* would definitely include women and aborigines, but who else would it include as far as the census is concerned? For example, does it include non-citizens, does it include new born babies, and are all children included as *"people"* in the context of the Constitution?

Seeing the Constitution, and the never-ending laws it allows the governments to make, does cover every single person living in Australia, it could be justified to say that *"people"* includes every living soul in Australia. Therefore, to obtain a number for the "quota" do we have to divide the total number of living souls in Australia by twice the number of Senators in the Senate?

Is this how it works, and is this the reason the Senate came first in the Constitution?

Or is the "quota" determined from the number of Australian citizens eligible to vote at whatever voting age applied at the time of the census?

Allocating House of Representative membership to the States

Subsection (ii) of **Section 24** sets out the method for determining the number of members each State shall be allowed for the House of Representative. The subsection reads:

(ii) the number of members to be chosen in each State shall be determined by dividing the number of the people of the State, as shown by the latest statistics of the Commonwealth, by the quota; and if on such division there is a remainder greater than one-half of the quota, one more member shall be chosen in the State.

Again, the term *"people"* is used without definition, but otherwise, the method is straightforward.

However, the last sentence of this **Section 24** adds an overriding condition to the calculation for State representation, *"But notwithstanding anything in this section, five members at least shall be chosen in each Original State"*.

While this may have had some relevance in 1900, it certainly wouldn't apply today.

The choice of *"five members"* as a minimum is a bit strange considering there was a minimum of six Senate members for each State. It must have been very obvious at the time that New South Wales and Victoria would dominate the House of Representatives irrespective of the membership of the lesser populated States.

Section 25 provides some clarification as to who can and cannot be counted in the census. The Section reads:

Provision as to races disqualified from voting

For the purposes of the last section, if by the law of any State all persons of any race are disqualified from voting at elections for the more numerous House of the Parliament of the State, then, in reckoning the number of the people of the State or of the

Commonwealth, persons of that race resident in that State shall not be counted.

When we think about this section, we must come to the conclusion it is both unfair and racist. As we know, South Australia and Western Australia did give the vote to some Aborigines in their local elections prior to Federation, although it is unclear if any other races were given a similar opportunity. It is difficult to find out exactly who were counted in the State census. If some States included Aborigines, and other didn't, this makes an unfair comparison in assessing the number of *"people"* for the purpose of calculating membership numbers.

This section also concedes that the State law is to be applied to the Commonwealth law for conducting a census.

Section 26 proceeds to override everything in **Section 24** by specifying the House of Representative members to be allocated to each State, but only for the first election under this new Constitution.

Overall, this is a very weird section because; it stipulates the number of members for the "Original" States, which as we have seen in the earlier lesson, does exclude Western Australia. Suddenly, there is a provision for counting Western Australia as an "Original" State.

Apart from this weird bit, the number of members for all the other "original" States, except Tasmania, is increased as a result of the inclusion of Western Australia in the list. What is the logic here, as the population of the "Original "States doesn't change when Western Australia is included?

	Initial allocation	Revised Allocation
New South Wales	23	26
Victoria	20	23
Queensland	9	9
South Australia	6	7
Tasmania	5	5
Western Australia	Nil	5

Although this is irrelevant in the current era, it is a second example of how dated this document really is. Had any Government in the past given some consideration to having a periodic review system in place, this document could have been kept up to date and made relevant by properly defining how the Government actually works.

Section 27 virtually overrides everything in the previous sections by giving Parliament an unqualified and unrestricted "power" to *"make laws for increasing or diminishing the number of the members of the House of Representatives"*.

As this section does not refer to any procedure set out in **Sections 24** and **25**, it is really a "blank cheque" for Parliament to do whatever they like, subject only to the agreement of the Senate.

However, as the Senate, then and especially now, has been converted to a political party House, a major change to the Constitution could easily be made if the ruling party were in control of both Houses.

This is a very dangerous Section as far as the integrity of the Constitution is concerned.

The only safeguard that would be available, should any Government try to manipulate the Constitution through this section, would be the necessary assent of the Governor General. He alone, according to the Constitution, is responsible for upholding the Constitution's integrity.

Section 28 is quite explicit in specifying that there shall be elections for the House of Representatives every 3 year period, *"but may be sooner (if) dissolved by the Governor-General"*.

The wording of this phrase is a little strange, as the word "if" is left out. This then puts the emphasis on the word "may". As we noted in an earlier lesson, "may" is often translated as "shall", but in this phrase it could be read as "can".

Are there any legal implications relating to this phrasing?

We learnt from **Section 5** that the Governor General has the authority to dissolve the House of Representatives and he can "prorogue" Parliament, **but there is no provision for him to dissolve the Senate.** Nor is there any explanation, or conditions, spelling out the grounds for which the Governor General can arbitrarily take this sort of drastic action. Obviously, as Commander in Chief of the Armed Forces, any such action he may choose to take would go unchallenged, as it would presumably be backed by the military.

Section 29 is actually quite an alarming section, as it gives the Commonwealth Parliament total control over how the States may choose to divide and allocate their allowed membership to the House of Representatives. The only apparent restriction is that divisions cannot overlap State borders, but a High Court could rule that this doesn't apply because of the words, *"until the Parliament of the Commonwealth otherwise provides".*

In reality, this Section could be construed for the purpose of "regionalising" Australia by ignoring State borders. Weakening and neutralising the concept of States, and State Governments, is something several Commonwealth Governments have unsuccessfully tried to do through having Local Government come under Commonwealth jurisdiction.

As there is no reference to Local Government in the Constitution, this third tier of government could only be added through a Referendum. The Commonwealth Government has tried to do this twice, and failed both times. If the Commonwealth Government had the power to control Local Government, they would be in the position to determine the borders of these local authorities, and under **Section 29**, those borders could extend beyond State borders.

Section 30 is another opportunity for the Commonwealth Government to alter the Constitution without going through the Referendum process. It again provides an unrestricted authority for the Commonwealth Government to manipulate the qualifications and laws that will apply to Federal elections.

Although the actual wording for this authority does use a phrase to imply a restriction; the phrase, *"but subject to this Constitution"* is actually quite meaningless, as it doesn't specify which parts of the Constitution would apply.

It is this type of wording that gives free rein to the High Court to interpret the Constitution in any way they so please, but in accordance to the politics of the times.

As this is another rather lengthy lesson, and there are ten more sections relating to setting up the House of Representatives, we will investigate those in the next lesson.

LESSON 9A

Section 31 Again, this section commences, *"Until the Parliament otherwise provides, but subject to this Constitution,…"* and it goes on to say that the State laws for the elections to their Legislative Assemblies shall apply to the election of the State's members for the House of Representatives. As with the last **Section 30**, the meaningless phrase, *"but subject to this Constitution"* is used without reference to any part of the Constitution.

This gives the Federal Parliament the authority create their own laws for the election of the State's membership to the House of Representatives. While this could lead to a uniformity in the election process, and counter the differences in the State laws, it could also lead to a conflict between two different systems.

What was the intent for giving Parliament the "power" to alter the Constitution?

If it was to provide uniformity, why wasn't this intent written into the Constitution as the condition which would be the *"subject to this Constitution"* provision?

We will probably never know the answer to that question, but in the meantime, Parliament has a free hand to do as they please.

Section 32 Suddenly, we are presented with a completely new and undefined entity – *"The Governor General in Council"*. What is this, who is on this Council, how many people are involved, and how is this entity supposed to take action?

Section 32 says: *"The Governor-General in Council **may** cause writs to be issued for general elections of members of the House of Representatives"*.

We again come across this curious use of the word *"may"*, which implies *"The Governor General in Council"* has an option to either issue a writ(s) or refuse to do so.

As we have noted before, "may" often seems to translate as "shall", which would seem the more appropriate intention. However, what is more intriguing is, why can't the Governor General act alone in issuing a writ(s)? Why must this mysterious "Council" be involved? And why do multiple "writs" need to be issued, or is the use of a plural simply a mistake?

The rest of the section is quite definite: *"After the first general election, the writs **shall** be issued within ten days from the expiry of a House of Representatives or from the proclamation of dissolution thereof"*. We notice that the word *"shall"* is particularly used in this case so, the distinction between *"shall"* and *"may"* is obviously recognised by the "founding fathers".

But again, we find some unusual terms, namely, *"the expiry of a House of Representatives"*. **Section 28** states quite clearly that the House of Representatives *"**shall** continue for three years"* unless the Governor General decides to dissolve it by issuing a proclamation.

If the three years is mandatory, as the Constitution says in **Section 28**, why isn't the "three years" related to the "expiry" in **Section 32**?

On checking our facts, we note that neither **Section 28**, nor **32**, is open to the Parliament's manipulation in being allowed to *"otherwise provide"*, hence, it would seem the *"three years"* is not set in concrete, if we are to apply **Section 32?**

Section 33 allows the "Speaker" of the House of Representatives to issue "his" writ for the election of a new member should a vacancy occur.

But, who or what is a "Speaker"? In **Section 35** we learn that "he" is a member of the House, but nowhere are "his" duties described, or how "he" is to be chosen.

We also notice that everything so far in this Constitution is referenced to the male gender, which of course, is a reflection of the day and age when the Constitution was written.

As an interesting anecdote, Julia Baird is working on a biography of Queen Victoria and found the following: All women in the Victorian era were taught to think of themselves as inferior, and men as their leaders. Victoria called Albert "Master"; he called her "Child."

In view of this obvious bias, and if the Constitution is to be applied as written, shouldn't it be necessary to have a Referendum to change the bias and include the female gender?

Unless that is done, in a strict legal sense, no women should be allowed to stand for a seat in the Federal Parliament.

Anyway, to review the rest of this **Section 33**, we find this mysterious entity, *"The Governor General in Council"* is also allowed to issue a writ **if there is no "Speaker",** or if the "Speaker" is absent. As with **Section 19**, this seems to imply the House of Representatives can operate without having a "Speaker" in place

Section 34 Once more we find this section starts with the catch all phrase, *"Until the Parliament otherwise provides",* but this time there is no reference to maintaining anything contained in the Constitution. As this deals with the qualifications for Members of the House of Representatives, it gives the political party in power at any given time, the authority to ignore, rescind, and revise any qualifications set out in this Constitution – and without the need to get the people's approval.

In a rational world, one would think that it is important the qualifications for any politician ought to be a matter of great concern to the general public.

If the people are going to elect someone to represent them, and allow that person to make laws to impact on everyone's life, surely the people have the right to demand certain basic qualifications, such as, honesty, no criminal convictions, no dual nationality, a proper knowledge of the Constitution, no conflict of interest, and a certain level of education? It goes without saying, that every member of the Parliament must be an Australian citizen and possibly within a minimum and/or maximum age range.

But of course, "the people" were never really part of this Constitution, or given serious consideration in the creation of the document.

Obviously, if the qualifications for politicians are left up to the political parties in Parliament, there is nothing to stop them from making sure every candidate is a member of an **approved** political party. What constitutes an **"approved"** political party is very much in the hands of the political party in charge of Parliament, and the government.

This Section 34 appears another very dangerous provision in the Constitution that could have serious repercussions for the people.

As the qualifications are described in Subsections (i) and (ii) in the Constitution, neither of the Subsections specifies the member must be a citizen of Australia.

The Subsections read:

(i) *he must be of the full age of twenty-one years, and must be an elector entitled to vote at the election of members of the House of Representatives, or a person qualified to become such elector, and must have been for three years at the least a resident within the limits of the Commonwealth as existing at the time when he is chosen;*

(ii) *he must be **a subject of the Queen,** either natural-born or for at least five years naturalized under **a law of the United Kingdom,** or of a Colony which has become or becomes a State, or of the Commonwealth, or of a State.*

Both these Subsections use the male gender, but this Subsection (ii) refers specifically to Queen Victoria, the British Monarch, and by tradition, her heirs and successors, also British. It therefore requires that any member of the Australian Parliament must be a British citizen, or "subject".

Under **Section 16**, the qualifications for members of the Senate are the same as those for the House of Representatives, and any changes that are subsequently introduced will impact on the Senate. This actually represents a peculiar situation. Any bill presented to the House of Representatives would have to be agreed by the Senate before it could become law, and by tying the changes to both Houses of Parliament could, as the "founders" well knew, be an issue of conflict. It can also as a valid check against the tyranny of a political party, but only if that party doesn't control both Houses of Parliament

Section 35 This is the section that introduces the unexplained position of a "Speaker" for the House of Representatives. The first business of the House at its first sitting after any election is to "choose" one of the members to become the "Speaker". How he is chosen and what his duties may be, are not mentioned.

As the wording of this section is very similar to the wording of **Section 17**, which deals with the "choosing" of a "President" of the Senate, we must assume the "Speaker" represents some form of leadership for the House of Representatives.

As there is no recognition of political parties in this original Constitution, one would think that a leader of the House ought to command a significant support from the other members, at least two thirds of the total membership.

But how are candidates chosen or nominated, and how do the other members have a say in the process?

The answer to these questions ought to be spelled out in the Constitution, if the people are to have any confidence that the leaders of the Houses of Parliament will be fair, unbiased and objective.

Section 36 is relatively straight forward in dealing with the absence of the "Speaker", except it says, *"the House of Representatives __may__ choose a member to perform his duties in his absence"*. Is it intended that the Constitution gives the House an option to operate without a "Speaker"? Or is this just semantics rather than a case of sloppy wording?

Section 37 simply says a member of the House can resign by sending a letter to the "Speaker", or in the Speaker's absence, addressed to the Governor General.

Section 38 is a direct copy of **Section 20** in Part II that deals with the Senate. It therefore raises exactly the same questions.

The confusion lies in the definition of the word, *"session"* – does this mean that a "session" lasts for two months or more, and the member has to miss a whole two months of sittings without permission before he's sacked?

Or does this mean that if he's absent for two consecutive months without permission, and doesn't attend any sessions of the House in that time, then there is grounds for dismissal?

If the Member were to attend only one day of a "session" in any two months, then this provision wouldn't apply. In other words, a Member need only attend six days of sessions in any twelve months to circumvent getting permission to be absent.

Alternatively, does *"session"* refer to the whole term of office for which a Member is elected? Another option is whether it refers to any twelve month period?

And why are the "sessions" related to "Parliament" rather than the House of Representatives? From our earlier investigation it appeared that "Parliament" refers to both the Houses of Parliament. The wording really doesn't make sense. A further anomaly arises from the words, *"without the permission of the House"*. How does "the House" give its permission? Why isn't it a duty of the "Speaker" to give permission, as distinct from the implication that all the other members of the House must be involved?

Section 39 This Section replicates the wording of **Section 22** dealing with a quorum for the Senate, and it uses the same one third of the elected members, but it too starts off with our familiar catch phrase, *"Until the Parliament otherwise provides"*. **Consequently, the same questions arise - The Section again sets an extremely low attendance for establishing a quorum, which by any rational measure should be at least fifty percent plus one, at a minimum. Better still; the quorum should be set at two thirds the total number of Members. Another anomaly arises with this section, as it creates a quite unnecessary complication. The actual wording reads,** *"Until the Parliament otherwise provides, the presence of at least one-third of the whole number of the members of the House of Representatives shall be necessary to constitute a meeting of the House for the exercise of its powers"*.

As we said before, the opening phrase, *"Until the Parliament otherwise provides,..."* specifically refers to the **Parliament**, but why is Parliament involved? Surely, this is a matter for the House to decide, and it shouldn't need to involve the Senate?

And what happens if the Senate tries to impose their wishes on the "lower" House, and that House rejects the amendment?

By using the word "Parliament", it signifies that both Houses must agree to any change.

On the other hand, specifying a quorum to legitimise the *"exercise of its powers"* is a very important issue that shouldn't be available to either the "Parliament", or the House of Representatives, to manipulate for the benefit of the politicians.

Most certainly, there should be a prohibition on reducing the numbers for a quorum below one third. By rights, the setting of a quorum should be a privilege of the people to decide, and not something that can safely be left in the hands of the "political party" that happens to be in power at any given time.

Section 40 deals with the voting in the House, and differs from the arrangement under **Section 23** for the Senate. In the case of a tie in the voting, the "Speaker" is given the "right" of a casting vote, which in the light of the known existence of political parties, is actually quite unfair.

The same arrangement as in the Senate should apply in the House, if there is a tie in the voting, the motion should pass in the negative. Decisions that are dependent on the vote of one person are obviously contentious, and do not have a clear support of the House.

This completes our investigation into Part III of the Constitution, and like all our earlier investigation, it continues to raise many questions about the way it is written.

As the Constitution is really all about the people of Australia, it ought to be a Constitution they can read and understand. It also needs to be a Constitution that describes things in the way the people actually want them to be.

What we have investigated so far certainly doesn't do that.

LESSON 10

Part IV – Both Houses of Parliament

This fourth Part of the Constitution appears to try and deal with the issues that are common to both Houses of Parliament. The first two **Sections, 41** and **42**, are straight forward, except for the aspects we need to investigate.

The Sections read:

Section 41 Right of electors of States

"No adult person who has or acquires a right to vote at elections for the more numerous House of the Parliament of a State shall, while the right continues, be prevented by any law of the Commonwealth from voting at elections for either House of the Parliament of the Commonwealth".

This is quite specific and does not make any provision for a Federal political party to tamper with the Constitution, but it does include a loophole with the words, *"while the right continues".* **The "right" it is referring to is a "right" conferred by the State.**

What if the political party in any of the States, and especially a State with only one House, were to restrict the "right" of its adults by setting certain specified qualifications? For example, a State Government could pass a law prohibiting any adult with a criminal conviction from voting in the State elections. There are numerous avenues available to a State

Government for denying people the "right" to vote, hence by tying this provision to the States it could lead to different and unfair voting provisions.

However, another problem seems to occur with this Section, as it could be in conflict with **Sections 10** and **30**, both of which do give Parliament the Constitutional authority to *"otherwise provide"* in respect to election of the members of both Houses. Those two sections would appear to completely override the **Section 41**, by virtue of a later **Section 109** that says Federal law will prevail over any State law if there is a conflict.

Section 42 Oath or affirmation of allegiance

"Every senator and every member of the House of Representatives shall before taking his seat make and subscribe before the Governor-General, or some person authorised by him, an oath or affirmation of allegiance in the form set forth in the schedule to this Constitution".

In order to assess the merits or otherwise of this section, we need to jump ahead to the Schedule and see what Oath, or Affirmation, the members are required to swear to.

The Schedule is as follows:

OATH

I, *A.B.*, do swear that I will be faithful and bear true allegiance to Her Majesty Queen Victoria, Her heirs and successors according to law. SO HELP ME GOD!

AFFIRMATION

I, *A.B.*, do solemnly and sincerely affirm and declare that I will be faithful and bear true allegiance to Her Majesty Queen Victoria, Her heirs and successors according to law.

(NOTE: *The name of the King or Queen of the United Kingdom of Great Britain and Ireland for the time being is to be substituted from time to time.*)

This is all very tricky in view of some of the actions taken by the Parliament, and particularly the High Court, in recent years. The above schedule in contained in the copy of the Constitution dated 25 July 2003 that is posted on the Internet by a Government website. The year 2003 is long after the Government took the extraordinary action in 1973 of changing the 1953 Royal Styles and Titles Act to rename *"Elizabeth the Second, by the Grace of God of the United Kingdom, Australia and her other Realms and Territories, Queen, Head of the Commonwealth, Defender of the Faith..."*. The Parliament changed the 1953 Act to become the 1973 Royal Styles and Tiles Act and renamed Elizabeth, *"Elizabeth the Second, Queen of Australia"*.

So, here we are thirtyone years later, still requiring the Australian members of Parliament to swear allegiance to the Queen of the UK.

Apart from this whole exercise in name changing being totally ludicrous, it is both illegal in terms of the UK's own laws for their Queen, and in conflict with Australia's own Royal Powers Act, which still refers to Queen Elizabeth the Second of the UK.

Seeing Australia has never had a Queen Elizabeth the First, how can we have a Queen Elizabeth the Second? And when was this newly formed Monarch of Australia ever coroneted in Australia and required to swear allegiance to the Australian people?

As far as the Government and the legal profession are concerned, these "nit-picking" questions are not worthy of an answer. Clearly, none of these people really consider Australia to be an independent, democratic nation, although they all hypocritically pay homage to the concepts.

An independent, democratic nation is one where the people are the fountainhead of all political power, and all politicians, public servants, judges and military personal, hold their positions through the authority of the people.

Thus any oath, or affirmation for office, must swear allegiance to the people of Australia, and uphold the principles and values contained in the Constitution as the primary law of the nation. It is essentially, an act of treason for any Australian citizen, ___if we were an independent, democratic Australia___, to swear allegiance to a foreign power, and deny swearing allegiance to the Australian people.

The act of "treason" is actually quite a complicated and subjective issue. The common definition of "treason" is *"The violation of allegiance to one's country"*, but if one's country is ruled by a dictator, or a government immersed in corruption, or repeatedly in breech of its Constitution, then surely one has a responsibility to act "treasonably" towards those in authority? Such action is really an act of patriotism towards one's country under those circumstances.

Even Professor Story in his book on the US Constitution relates "treason" to any person who *"aims at the overthrow of the government"*, but on the other side of the coin, he says a government has a duty and responsibility to ensure its survival and stability. It is this last assertion that supports the existence of coercive and repressive governments, against which an *"act of treason"* could be seen as a courageous and patriotic act of defiance. In the eyes of a government, perpetrators of this latter action are seen as "traitors", and as has become more common today, as "whistleblowers".

How one sees the act of "treason" seems to depend on which side of the fence one sits.

Section 43 is another example of 'sloppy' writing as it leaves out an obvious condition. The section makes the statement, *"A member of either House of the Parliament shall be incapable of being chosen or of sitting as a member of the other House"*.

This bald statement implies that anyone elected to either House of Parliament is forever prohibited from standing for the other House at any time in the future. That is clearly ridiculous, and we know it has not been followed in practice. The missing condition should be the four words, *"at the same time"*.

Section 44 is a very important section that was designed to protect the integrity of Parliament by ensuring every elected member is not tainted by allegiance to any foreign authority, or open to a conflict of interest, either monetary or commercial.

The sad part of this section is that it has been continually observed in the breach of the conditions. We know this for a fact, from the amendments to the Common Informers Act in 1975, but obviously, this section has been ignored for a long time before that.

In 1999, when the High Court, in a split decision, decided that Britain was a "foreign country in the Sue v Hill case, they thereby denied Heather Hill her election to the Senate, as she hadn't completed her renunciation of her British passport. At the time, there were twentyeight known members of Parliament holding dual passports, and none were expelled, despite the High Court ruling that they were in breach of Section 44(i).

Section 44(i) reads:

Any person who:

(i) is under any acknowledgment of allegiance, obedience, or adherence to a foreign power, or is a subject or a citizen or entitled to the rights or privileges of a subject or a citizen of a foreign power; or......

shall be incapable of being chosen <u>or of sitting</u> as a senator or a member of the House of Representatives.

There are four other conditions that prohibit people from holding a seat in Parliament, but there are some special conditions attached to subsection (iv) that allows discriminatory privilege to some, as yet, unidentified members of Parliament, called "Ministers" and also to members of the armed forces.

Subsection (iv) reads: *"holds any office of profit under the Crown, or any pension payable during the pleasure of the Crown out of any of the revenues of the Commonwealth; or …"*

The discriminatory exception reads: *But subsection (iv) does not apply to the office of any of the Queen's Ministers of State for the Commonwealth, or of any of the Queen's Ministers for a State, or to the receipt of pay, half pay, or a pension, by any person as an officer or member of the Queen's navy or army, or to the receipt of pay as an officer or member of the naval or military forces of the Commonwealth by any person whose services are not wholly employed by the Commonwealth."*

The way this exception is written is a bit curious, to say the least.

Why are *"the Queen's Ministers for a State,"* included when **Section 44** specifically deals with members of the Federal Parliament?

Does this mean that a State Minister can also hold a seat in the Federal Parliament and not lose any remuneration he gets from his State position?

Or does this imply a State Minister could hold a Federal Seat at the same time?

Also, the wording of the last part of this long sentence is difficult to understand. The sentence differentiates between *"the Queen's navy or army"* and *"an officer or member of the naval or military forces of the Commonwealth"*, but then adds this strange bit at the end *"by any person whose services are not wholly employed by the Commonwealth."*

Who do they mean by *"any person"*? Does this refer to military personal, and if they are *"not wholly employed by the Commonwealth"*, would this include foreign mercenaries?

Again, the antiquated and out of date nature of this section provides support for a logical and rational periodic Constitutional review process that could keep the Constitution up to date. In that event, it would be prudent to include the Air Force, something that didn't exist in 1900.

Subsection (v) is another one that causes some concern. It reads:

(v) has any direct or indirect pecuniary interest in any agreement with the Public Service of the Commonwealth otherwise than as a member and in common with the other members of an incorporated company consisting of more than twenty-five persons;

The exception, as noted with the word *"otherwise"*, seems to say that any employee of an incorporated company with more then twentyfive employees can become a member of Parliament whether or not there is *"any direct or indirect pecuniary interest"*. Any similar employee of a smaller company with less than twentyfive employees would be prohibited.

This either doesn't make sense, or it is deliberately included in the Constitution to allow Directors, and senior personal from the larger companies, to be elected to Parliament. This would seem very much a case of the Colonial "aristocracy" looking after their own interests.

Section 45 is both specific and peculiar at the same time. In 3 subsections it spells out certain of the breaches for the conditions detailed in **Section 44**, and sets the punishment for these breaches as dismissal from Parliament. However, what it doesn't do is define how these breaches are dealt with in terms of proving them, and who determines the process of disqualification.

A disqualification process is a very serious issue, both for the member and the integrity of the Parliamentary system, and one would think a Constitution should clearly set out the guidelines, at least, for what sort of process needs to be followed. This issue has the potential for ramifications, not only in respect to further criminal indictment, but also the possibility of retrospectivity in laws that involved the participation of the subsequently disqualified member.

Section 46 is another of these very peculiar sections in that it deals with a situation, which according to **Section 45** cannot exist. If a member of either House is disqualified, under **Sections 45**, and presumably **Section 44**, (although that is not clearly spelled out) the seat becomes vacant, and the elected member can no longer sit in Parliament.

This **Section 46** reads: *"Until the Parliament otherwise provides, any person declared by this Constitution to be incapable of sitting as a senator or as a member of the House of Representatives shall, for every day on which he so sits, be liable to pay the sum of one hundred pounds to any person who sues for it in any court of competent jurisdiction".*

The obvious problem are lies in the words *"declared by this Constitution..."* because, a piece of paper cannot take action to disqualify a Member of Parliament.

Some formal process has to be set up to examine the circumstances and determine if the Constitution has been breached to the extent that disqualification is justified.

As the Constitution does not set up this process, and this particular section starts with our familiar *"Until the Parliament otherwise provides"*, it is apparent that "Parliament" has completely reneged on their responsibility to implement the required process.

That is probably the reason why twentyeight members of Parliament were allowed to continue in office as of 1999 while holding dual passports and allegiance to foreign countries.

There is another problem regarding the definition of terms. What constitutes *"any court of competent jurisdiction"*? Who decides which courts are competent to hear any claims? As it is a Constitutional matter, does this involve the High Court and the massive costs that would entail?

As it happens, those questions are all academic anyway because, our politicians were not content with simply ignoring a disqualification process, and they were determined to totally gut the penalty provisions of this section. They used the loophole phrase of the opening sentence to amend their earlier law and create a new one called, "The Common Informers (Parliamentary Disqualifications) Act 1975", They adding a Section 4 to read: *"On and after the date of commencement of this Act, a person is not liable to pay any sum under **Section 46** of the Constitution and no suit shall be instituted, continued, heard or determined in pursuance of that Section."*

To make matters worse, the Governor General gave assent to this law on April 23rd 1975, in total disregard to the effect it had in altering the Constitution. As with so many other anomalies related to this Constitution, there appeared no restriction on how many 'persons' could sue any declared disqualified member, but the 1975 legislation restricted the action to a single person.

It is interesting to note that according to the Australian Bureau of Statistics Inflation calculator, one hundred pounds a day in 1901 is roughly equivalent to fifteen thousand dollars per day in today's currency.

Section 47 should totally nullify the High Court decision in the 1999 case of Sue v Hill as this Section says *"any question of a disputed election to either House, shall be determined by the House in which the question arises"*.

However, our "founding fathers" must have had some experience with disputed elections because, they saw fit to slip in their wonderful little catch all phrase *"Until the Parliament otherwise provides"*, thus allowing the Howard Government to palm off the Heather Hill/One Nation problem to the High Court.

But that phrase didn't just cover the situation of disputed elections, it also covered questions related to the qualifications of elected members, and also issues dealing with any vacancy that occurs.

Possibly, the government could have used this section in 1977 to ensure vacancies are filled by members from the same political party, thus avoiding the cost of a referendum to change **Section 15**.

Section 48 Once more the catch phrase is used to allow Parliament to change the wording of the Constitution, but in this case there is a certain amount of justification for its application. **Section 48** says that all the members of the Senate and the House of Representatives shall be paid the same amount of *"allowance"*, which in 1900, was fixed at four hundred pounds a year. According to the Bureau's inflation calculation, that is equivalent to roughly $57,000 in today's money.

A point worth noting is the annual remuneration of ten thousand pounds for the Governor General in 1900 compared to the four hundred pounds for a Member of Parliament. (Which at that time would also include a member to act as our unmentioned, and technically, unconstitutional, "Prime Minister") We must wonder whether this ratio between the "allowances" has been maintained. It is interesting to note there is no reference to any special *"allowance"* for the President of the Senate or the Speaker of the House. Nor is there any reference to these mysterious "Ministers," first mentioned in **Section 44**.

Obviously, the *"till Parliament otherwise provides"* will do the trick and allow the "pollies" to set themselves up nicely.

Section 49 is an absolute disaster for the people of Australia, but it is a goldmine for the politicians. This section is the open door for incorporating the Westminster system into how Australia is governed. It is probably the most powerful section in the whole Constitution, as it is the very crux of what the "people" should have the total authority to determine.

The *"**powers, privileges, and immunities**"* of a Government system are the critical foundation for creating a Constitution in the first place. To hand this over to the politicians is a travesty for any democratic aspirations of the people.

It gives the politicians "open slather" to set up their *"**powers, privileges, and immunities** of the Senate and of the House of*

Representatives, _and of the members_ and the committees of each House, shall be such _as are declared by the Parliament......"._

The only temporary hitch is that they have to follow the _"powers, privileges, and immunities"_ used in the UK until the Parliament declare their own in Australia.

As it turned out, this wasn't a temporary hitch at all because; the Australia Parliament adopted and maintained, virtually the entire Westminster system as it applied in the UK.

This section is the one that establishes and maintains the status quo, which was the real goal of the "founding fathers", and they hid it midway in the Constitution with this apparent innocuous wording.

In respect to the welfare and authority for the people of Australia, this has to be the most terrible section in the whole of the Constitution.

Section 50 answers the question as to what is meant by _"declared by the Parliament"._

It allows each House to determine their own _"**powers, privileges, and immunities**"_ which is a devastating proposal as there is no suggestion of coordination between the separate Houses of Parliament.

Our investigation of the Constitution has led us to this monumental discovery, that the "founding fathers" always intended Australia would adopt the Westminster system of Government. It was the only system they knew, and it is a system that operates on a massive number of unwritten, uncodefied, conventions, all largely unknown to the general public.

But is this really the foundation the people want for an independent and democratic Australia? Or do we want an Australia where the people are the fountainhead of all political "power" – where the people say what sort of government they

97

really want – and what sort of authority they are prepared to allow their delegated representatives?

Obviously, none of that is going to happen under this present Constitution because, it was written entirely for the politicians and public servants of the day, to enshrine the system they had used, and intended to continue to use for the "indissoluble' life of the newly formed federated Colony of the Commonwealth of Australia.

LESSON 11

Part V Powers of the Parliament

Section 51, is the first Section in Part V of Clause 9 in the British law to establish the federated colony to be known as the Commonwealth of Australia. The section provides a fairly comprehensive list of the responsibilities and duties which are entrusted to this newly formed entity. It commences with our now familiar phrase, *"The parliament shall ....have power ...."*, but they throw in the quaint little condition *"....subject to this Constitution...."*, without offering any reference to which parts of the Constitution these "powers" will be *"subject to"*. One can presume this meaningless condition is included to give the false impression that there are some limitations on the subsequent list of thirtynine functions for which the Federal Government is given responsibility.

What are the Constitutional limitations on the Federal Government?

In fact, there are limitations on the Federal Government, but these limitations only come from two sources. The first source comes from what is **not included** in the Constitution, and the thirtynine functions listed in **Section 51** includes some that are quite specific, while others are rather nebulous and open to a variety of interpretations.

The second limitation is actually not in this Constitution, but it comes from whatever the High Court decides doesn't apply to the Federal Government. As we noted above, the High Court uses their unconstitutional prerogative of what they call, "judicial review" to interpret the words of the Constitution in any way it suits them. Thus, while this might be a limitation on some occasions, on others, it can represent "open slather" for the Federal Government.

Other than that, the Federal Government is given a free hand to alter and manipulate the Constitution in any way it pleases them. They can do this through courtesy of the "founding fathers" inserting their perennial little catch phrase, *"until Parliament otherwise provides"*, or words of similar effect.

Another little anomaly

The opening sentence of Section 51 gives the Parliament the power *"to make laws for the peace, order and good government of the Commonwealth ...."*

What is not generally known is that the original wording used the word *"welfare"* rather than *"order"* in this sentence. Obviously, there is a huge difference between looking after the "welfare" of the something compared to maintaining "order" in that something. In a sense, this probably doesn't matter in this case because the only "something" for which both "welfare" and "order" can apply is to the "Commonwealth". The Constitution is not really concerned with the "welfare" of the people, but it definitely does have a very strong interest in maintaining the "welfare" of the Commonwealth, especially against anything that might threaten the Government and the "establishment". By the same token, every Government has a strong vested interest in maintaining "order" to ensure the status quo in maintained, and the people are never in a position to threaten the system.

The other undefined words in these opening sentences are, *"good government"*. Good government from whose perspective – the political party in power, the vested interests of the commercial and financial sectors, the maintenance of the status quo, or at the bottom end of the queue, "the people"? There are huge gaps in the philosophies that apply to *doing good*" for each of the groups in that shortened list. They range from profit at any cost under a "free market" capitalist philosophy, to the domination of the financial interests by controlling the money supply, to a mixed economy of Government and private ownership, to a totalitarian tyranny with the Government in full control, or a Government with a philosophy that puts the people first and the political party second.

It is this question of philosophy that really conditions the purpose of a Constitution, how it is written, and equally as important, how it is interpreted and applied.

The list of specific Federal Government "responsibilities"

Having investigated the opening sentence of this important **Section 51**, we can now continue the examination of the thirtynine functions included in the list. Some of these functions are logical and straight forward, but others are quite questionable in terms of their wording, their implication, and especially in the way they have been used in the course of the last one hundred and fourteen years. This has amounted to manipulating the Constitution to suit the pragmatic expediency of the times.

The first function is:

> (i) *trade and commerce with other countries, and among the States;* at face value, this seems a logical function, and in truth, so it is. However, what it does do is emphasise the importance of the "economy" in relation to this new federated colony. By placing this issue first and foremost in the list of the Commonwealth's "responsibilities" it says that trade

and commerce are the lifeblood of the federation. What this "responsibility" also does is to establish the fact that the Commonwealth will operate on the basis of a "controlled economy" with the government making the laws on how trade and commerce will be conducted. As this federated colony is to be *"indissoluble"* this government "responsibility" means there can never be any such thing as "free enterprise" or a "free market", as the government will always be in control, unless for some inexplicable reason, it chooses otherwise.

(ii) *taxation; but so as not to discriminate between States or parts of States;* this imposition is simply a carry over from centuries of tradition in enforcing the people to suffer the burden of paying taxes. The purpose of this imposition has always been for maintaining the monarchy, the aristocracy, or other rulers, in the lifestyle they have grown up to expect and demand. In other words, this "responsibility" of the government ensures the people will always remain in servitude to those in "power", and that the status quo of the feudal traditions will be maintained. Throughout our recorded history, in virtually every occasion, "power" has come out of the barrel of a gun (or the tip of sword in earlier times). Even in a "democracy" there is always a "gun" at the bottom of a "public servant's" filing basket.

There is a glaring omission in placing taxation at the top of this list, because, the Constitution makes no provision for defining what is to be used for paying these taxes. If taxes are to be paid in "money"; where is this "money" coming from?

This is a hugely important question because; it really determines the whole economic future of the nation.

We will provide the proper answer in Lesson 15.

However, it is nice to know the federal government is, supposedly, not allowed to "discriminate" in the way they apply taxes to the States. As this function does not explain whether it is talking about the way taxes are imposed on the States, or whether it is talking about the way the taxes are spent in relation to the States, the bald statement is a bit like an open cheque. As we will find out, this "open cheque" has been used in many different ways, and has resulted in numerous court battles regarding its interpretation.

(iii) bounties on the production or export of goods, but so that such bounties shall be uniform throughout the Commonwealth; if taxes, under whatever name they are given, are to be imposed, it does make sense that, at the very least, they should be uniform throughout the Commonwealth. But uniform in what sense? Uniform as a percentage or uniform as a fixed amount? This could make a huge difference on the bounties collected from each State.

(iv) borrowing money on the public credit of the Commonwealth; this is another function of the government which perpetuates the existing traditions of the times, and indirectly, maintains the domination of the financial system, and the financial fraternity, over the government. However, there are two pertinent issues with this function. First, it recognises the existence of *"public credit"*, which in the nineteenth century was never seen as

being the property of "the people". *"Public credit"* was always seen as the power of the government to impose taxes on the people, by force if necessary. No government ever recognised that it was always the expenditure of effort and enterprise by the people that creates the ability to pay taxes in the first place. In that sense, *"public credit"*, in truth, is always a creation of "the people".

The second issue is to ask the question we raised above in subsection (ii) – where does this "money" come from that the Government needs to borrow?

Borrowing money seems to be a direct contradiction of function *(xii)*, which gives the government the power to make laws in relation to *"currency, coinage, and legal tender"*. In other words, the Commonwealth Government has the sole authority to create all the *"currency, coinage, and legal tender"* that this new federated colony might ever need. As this is truly the case, there is no need to borrow funds from any private source at all. Similarly, it also raises the question of whether the government needs to impose any taxes as well.

This function (xii) gives the Commonwealth a status of monetary sovereignty, which we will look at in Lesson 15.

(v) postal, telegraphic, telephonic, and other like services; communication is, and always has been, a vital factor for any society, and in the nineteenth century, the services contained in this subsection (v) were seen as a direct government responsibility. Obviously, with the emphasis placed on the economy, good communication was essential for all forms of commerce, and no less important from the

aspect of defence. On this occasion, the "founding fathers" did exhibit a bit of foresight outside of their political aims, by including the words, *and other like services*". This covers the huge revolution in communication, right up to the present day, but a revolution no one could have envisaged in the nineteenth century.

(vi) *the naval and military defence of the Commonwealth and of the several States, and the control of the forces to execute and maintain the laws of the Commonwealth;* while it is logical that the government should be able to recommend the management of the naval and military forces to the Commander in Chief, the wording of this subsection is ambiguous. It does not differentiate between military and civil *"forces"* in executing and maintaining the law. With the Governor General as Commander in Chief of all the military forces, this subsection reinforces his dictatorial position that would allow him to use the military for maintaining civil law and order.

Whilst the government may make draft bills to cover this subsection, those bills would only become law with the assent of the Governor General. Obviously, no Governor General in his right mind is going to give assent to any law that interferes with the Monarch's delegated responsibility as Commander in Chief.

The federal government would be able to make laws for establishing a civilian police force to *"execute and maintain laws of the Commonwealth"*, but this would not impact on any State laws policed by the State, unless there is a conflict between the State and Commonwealth laws.

(vii) *lighthouses, lightships, beacons and buoys;* this is an obvious responsibility to delegate to a federal government in the interest of uniformity, and the growing necessity for these installations.

(viii) *astronomical and meteorological observations;* again, another obvious delegation that would lead to the collation of State data to provide better, and more accurate information, on the nation's weather patterns.

(ix) *quarantine;* this too is a responsibility that needs to be implemented uniformly by each State to prevent the introduction of undesirable elements into Australia.

(x) *fisheries in Australian waters beyond territorial limits;* this is rather strange wording because, it seems to restrict the Commonwealth Government to only making laws for fishing in international waters. From this, we would assume that the States retain the right to make laws for *"fisheries"* in the Australian waters associated with their boundaries. The wording also implies that the Commonwealth Government would not be involved in any disputes related to fishing practices in Australian waters.

Also, the word *"fisheries"* is open to several interpretations. The Australian Government would certainly have the authority to make laws regarding *"fishing practices"* in international waters, but only to the extent it applies to Australian registered, or based, fishing vessels. The government could possibly regulate the size and type of catches from international waters, and even how those catches can be processed.

However, subsection (i) does give the Commonwealth Government control over any type of import or export business related to State *"fisheries"*. This could provide considerable control over the State's *"fisheries"* industry if it operates in these markets. A State's domestic operations and market appear not to come under Commonwealth control, but that is probably challengeable under subsection (i).

(xi) *census and statistics;* is a logical responsibility to hand over to the Commonwealth Government, particularly as it would provide uniformity in how the census is conducted, and exactly who and what is counted.

(xii) *currency, coinage, and legal tender;* as we noted above, this responsibility is probably the most useful and most important responsibility in this whole list. What it does, is to confer **monetary sovereignty** to the authority of the Commonwealth Government.

Most people, politicians and lawyers, then and now, have absolutely no understanding of what **monetary sovereignty** means or entails.

What monetary sovereignty means is that the Commonwealth Government has the sole authority to declare what will be considered as Australia's legal tender. And that includes every single dollar issued by the private banks in the form of loans, mortgages, credit, overdrafts, or any other form of dollar designated instrument.

The ramifications of this are immense, but the Australian government has only once in the last one hundred and fourteen years, used this authority properly, for the short twelve year period from 1911 to 1923. That was when they set up the original Commonwealth Bank of Australia and operated it as the nation's bank for the people of Australia.

We will provide a detailed discussion of monetary sovereignty, and especially the resounding success of the original Commonwealth Bank, in Lesson 15.

(xiii) *banking, other than State banking; also State banking extending beyond the limits of the State concerned, the incorporation of banks, and the issue of paper money;* this responsibility should be considered the second most important in this list, as it follows on from the declaration of monetary sovereignty, and provides the necessary regulatory authority over the private banking industry.

This delegation of authority has two other ramifications that have never been properly understood, or if they have been understood, they have been deliberately ignored. The first is the reference to *"the issue of paper money"*. Every single dollar issued in the form of *"paper money"* has to be legal tender, and as such, can only be issued by the Commonwealth Government. The most pertinent issue related to the creation of *"paper money"* in this Constitution is the total lack of any reference to "gold" and the nation's money supply. The issues relating to "gold" and the money supply have historical roots and need to be examined more fully, which we will also do in Lesson 15.

The second very significant ramification of this delegated authority is the Constitutional exclusion that prohibits the Commonwealth Government from interfering in any State banking that is confined within the State borders. What is important about this is the fact that any State Government could set up their own State bank and operate it in the same manner as the private banks. This means the State

Government could use the fractional reserve system to expand their bank's capital by ten or twelve times the deposited amount, and they could do it at a very low rate of interest to cover the operations of the bank.

While the State Governments do not have "monetary sovereignty", as neither do any of the private banks, the conventional fractional reserve system would allow the State to create their required "credit" facilities in exactly the same way as the private banks operate. This issue of the fractional reserve system also has historical roots and requires a detailed examination if we are to properly understand how it works.

This too will be discussed in Lesson 15.

As this has developed into a lengthy lesson, we will continue our examination of the remaining delegated responsibilities in the next lesson

LESSON 11A

This lesson is a continuation of the investigation into the remaining "responsibilities", which the colonial governments of the nineteenth century, were prepared to delegate to a centralised Commonwealth Government. These "responsibilities" stemmed purely from an agreement between the separate colonial governments about what "powers" they were prepared to cede to a central government. The will of "the people" was never considered in the formation of the Commonwealth Government. The very fact that the Westminster system of Government never gets a mention anywhere in the Constitution is proof that "the people" were never party to the creation of the document.

The next responsibility is subsection (xiv), which is similar to subsection (xiii)

> (xiv) *insurance, other than State insurance; also State insurance extending beyond the limits of the State concerned;* both this subsection and the previous one, comply with the colonial government's interest in protecting their own banking and insurance businesses from outside interference by the federal government. The colonies were prepared to concede a level of interference when the businesses extended beyond the colonial borders. However, it is completely open to a wide interpretation as to what constitutes, *"extending beyond the limits of the State concerned".* Could this be construed as an interstate person

receiving a benefit or payment, from a colonial business that has no branches outside of the colony?

As the Constitution is seen purely as a legal document, almost exclusively it is left up to the courts to decide how the words are interpreted. In that respect, the "people" have absolutely no say in what meaning or intent, they may wish to apply to the Constitution, except for the usually futile avenue of a court challenge, and at considerable expense.

(xv) *weights and measures;* this responsibility of the federal government is certainly a logical and appropriate one, as uniformity in weights and measures is an essential factor in all areas of commerce, and the daily lives of the people.

(xvi) *bills of exchange and promissory notes;* while these things are primarily related to commercial transactions, there is a need to ensure commitments are honoured, and there are legitimate avenues available to address any disputes that might arise.

(xvii) *bankruptcy and insolvency;* these issues are also closely linked to commercial activities, and they invariably result in a disadvantage to someone or some organisation. It is logical that any laws relating to either of these issues should be uniform throughout the Commonwealth, as interstate involvement could often be a factor.

(xviii) *copyrights, patents of inventions and designs, and trade marks;* again, there is a logical reason for adopting uniformity in these measures, especially where interstate trade is involved. It also absolves the States of a lot of administrative work and expenses by handing it over to the Commonwealth Government.

(xix) *naturalization and aliens;* as the colonies/States have now agreed to form a single united colony, the issue

of naturalisation means that a person so naturalised, becomes a citizen of the Commonwealth of Australia. Similarly, anyone declared an "alien" is alien to the Commonwealth and the British monarchy, as all Australian citizens, native born or naturatised, were considered to be British subjects.

(xx) *foreign corporations, and trading or financial corporations formed within the limits of the Commonwealth;* this subsection ties in with subsection (i) which could be interpreted as including foreign and financial corporations. The purpose for specifying these in a separate subsection is not clear; unless it is meant to provide for special conditions relating to UK owned businesses. That is probably not a valid explanation because, the UK was not then, and in fact even now, cannot be considered a "foreign country" while we continue to use their law as our Constitution. And that is despite anything the High Court of Australia might think or say. Their 1999 decision in so defining the UK as a "foreign country" was clearly wrong. It was illegally promulgated as a purely political decision; it has no ethical or moral basis in law, but as we know, ethics and morality do not hinder legal decisions.

(xxi) *marriage;* uniformity in marriage laws within the Commonwealth is a valid responsibility, although in the light of multiculturalism, and the changing norms of the society, this subsection should now be expanded to specifically include the marriage customs of other groups, races and nationalities, provided those customs conform to accepted Australian practices regarding age, prohibiting forced marriages, and other such criteria. If such an expansion in the definition of *"marriage"* were to be adopted, ethically, it should be done by way of a Referendum and not left to the whims of any political party that happens to be *"in power"* at any given time.

(*xxii*) *divorce and matrimonial causes; and in relation thereto, parental rights, and the custody and guardianship of infants;* the conflict that can arise from these issues could become more complex if each State were to apply their own laws, hence, it makes sense to delegate this responsibility to the Federal Government in the name of uniformity. There are three contentious points with the wording of this subsection; the first being in specifying *"parental rights"* but ignoring *"children's rights"*. The second contentious point is that this is one of the very few recognitions that there are any *"rights"* applying to anyone other than the Queen, in this Constitution, albeit, only to parents in this case.

The Question of "Rights"

In the whole of this Commonwealth Constitution the recognition that a person living in the Commonwealth of Australia has any form of individual *"rights"* occurs only twice, once in Section 41 regarding the "right" to vote, and in Section 51(xxii) where the parents are granted an undefined "right". The truth concerning "rights" is that they are only protected under the original colonial/State Constitutions, which were prohibited from making laws repugnant to the laws of England. Thus, the English Bill of Rights applied to the residents in each colony/State. The Westminster Act of 1942, and the Australia Act of 1986, both attempted to remove this protection, as well as trying to make many other changes to the Constitution. Hence, despite trying to impose these Acts under Section 51, subsection (xxxviii), both Acts needed to be passed at a Referendum before they could become law. No Referendums were ever called, and as a result, both Acts are legally ultra vires, and cannot, or should not apply in law.

The fact that the "rights" of the people is never mentioned in the Commonwealth Constitution is actually an understandable and deliberate omission. In the nineteenth century the concept of individual rights for ordinary people simply did not exist in the minds of government and bureaucratic people. That is despite the existence of the Habeas Corpus Act, and the British Bill of Rights, which then and now, are primarily observed, if at all, in principle rather than practice.

The third contentious point is the lack of any means for defining these *"rights"* which the Constitution allocates to "parents". The logical assumption in answer to this question is that the Federal Government has the sole jurisdiction in defining these *"rights"*. Thus, by implication, which is considered a legitimate legal process by the High Court of Australia, (see subsection (xxxix)) the definition and allocation of all *"rights"* could be deemed to be within the authority of any government of the day.

In reality, all "rights" are the property of the people, and they are never the property of any government or any court, in saying what "rights" the people may or may not have. However, a "right' only exists as long as it can be sustained, but in a "Democracy" it is always up to the people to decide which "rights" they wish to maintain and hold inviolate from any government, any person, or any organisation. If the people cannot do this then they are living under a tyranny.

> (xxiii) *invalid and old-age pensions;* while this is included as a federal responsibility, it is not, as many people like to believe, any sort of *"right"* bequeathed to the people. As long as these *"pensions"* are defined under legislation they can be allocated in any manner as

decided by any government of the day. It should be up to the Constitution to specifically define the nature and application of *"pensions"* through a set of guidelines that can only be amended via a Referendum.

(xxiiiA) the provision of maternity allowances, widows' pensions, child endowment, unemployment, pharmaceutical, sickness and hospital benefits, medical and dental services (but not so as to authorize any form of civil conscription), benefits to students and family allowances; (Added in 1946 by Referendum) While this added subsection greatly widens the scope of federal responsibility for numerous other pensions and allowances, it throws in an apparently unrelated phrase in the form of *"but not so as to authorize any form of civil conscription"*. On the assumption that everything is done for a reason, why is this unrelated phrase included in this added subsection?

What exactly is meant by the term *"civil conscription"?* Does this mean that civilians can not be conscripted for military service, and why isn't this very important provision allocated its own specific subsection? Bear in mind that this phrase was added as a result of the 1946 Referendum, when Australia had just survived the second World War. Was the intention to ensure no future Government would be allowed to implement enforced conscription of any civilians for any purpose?

This seems too important an issue to be *"slipped in"* as an apparent afterthought to the otherwise seemingly unrelated issue of pensions and allowances. Surely, the intention wasn't to say that no one should ever be "forced" to accept any of these allowances and benefits?

(xxiv) *the service and execution throughout the Commonwealth of the civil and criminal process and the judgments of the courts of the States;* this is an extremely wide ranging delegation of authority, and would seem to be in direct conflict with the powers and authority that the State Governments grant to their Police forces and court system. This subsection implies that the federal government has over riding control of all *"civil and criminal process and the judgments of the courts of the States"*.

From the people's point of view, whom should be the rightful owners of any Constitution, do they really want the federal government to have overriding control of all *"civil and criminal process and the judgments of the courts of the States"*. If a person has to first go through the State's "justice system" only to find that the Federal Government has overriding jurisdiction, doesn't this represent an unwarranted money making scheme for the legal system?

Logically, this subsection should come under Chapter III dealing with the Judicature. Also, the extent of coverage conveyed in these few words is so vast, that the ramifications of its implementation should be carefully thought out in terms of its Constitutional significance.

There is some justification in having uniformity in the laws, but as long as each State Parliament has a degree of autonomy in creating laws for its own State, delivering uniformity would be a bureaucratic nightmare.

Chapter V, which deals with the States, does provide in **Section 109** that the laws of the Commonwealth will prevail if there is any conflict with a State law.

The singular, most developed purpose of **EVERY** Parliament is the creation of a never ending stream of "laws". The ultimate aim is to control the lives of every person living in the nation. As a result, **Section 109** represents a financial goldmine for the legal profession should anyone claim a conflict between the State law and some Commonwealth law. The corollary to this is that every State law remains valid until it goes through an expensive legal process of being challenged in relation to a Commonwealth law.

(xxv) *the recognition throughout the Commonwealth of the laws, the public Acts and records, and the judicial proceedings of the States;* this subsection raises a couple of questions. First, what is meant by the word *"recognition"?* Another question is, "What is the purpose behind this *"recognition"?* Thirdly, to whom is the "recognition" supposed to apply? Is it intended to apply to the legal profession, or is the onus placed on the general public to "recognise" every one of the extensive list of *"laws, the public Acts and records, and the judicial proceedings of the States"?* Why is this a matter for a Constitution, especially as there is no indication of the purpose, or intended use of this information in the subsection? Is this part of the perpetuation of the established legal system that can pick and choose precedents from some obscure source, and apply it under different circumstances, conditions and time frame? Surely this is a straightforward bureaucratic or administrative matter that could be dealt with under legislation?

The anomalous nature of this "responsibility" prompted some research, and we find this wording is taken directly from the US Constitution. However, the very important condition relating to the intent and purpose of the text is left out. The missing words necessary to make sense of this subsection are contained in Professor Story's 1840 book. The words are, *"And the Congress may, by general laws, prescribe the manner, in which such acts, records, and proceedings **shall be proved, and the effect thereof**"*.

In other words, nothing can be taken as *"recognised"* until is certified and proven valid and applicable. So much for the astuteness of our "founding fathers" when they plagiarise only a part of the US Constitution, and clearly don't understand the significance of what they are plagiarising.

(xxvi) *the people of any race, ~~other than the aboriginal race in any State,~~ for whom it is deemed necessary to make special laws;* the deleted section of this sentence is part of the despicable way the government presents referendum questions. They play on what they perceive to be the sentiment of the population to add other amendments in the hope they will be approved without close scrutiny. This was the case in 1967 when ninety point seventyseven percent of the population agreed to delete the **Section 127**, from the Constitution. That referendum has been touted as Australia's most "successful" referendum, but it's "success" only occurred because the population were appalled to find how totally racist the "founding fathers" really were by declaring aborigines were not to be counted in the census.

However, by also deleting the words, *"other than the aboriginal race in any State"*, it effectively gave the Commonwealth Government the green light to create a whole new bureaucratic department to take over the administration of all aborigine affairs in Australia. Whether this is a good or bad thing isn't the issue; the issue is that the people were not told the intent behind deleting these words, and the ramifications for greatly increasing the governments "power" in this area. The referendum did not deny the States from making laws to administer aborigine affairs within their respective State borders, but the eventual outcome was a duplication of roles and the creation of conflicting policies.

(*xxvii*) *immigration and emigration;* while at first glance this might be seen as a logical delegation of responsibilities, it really should not have been handed over without specified qualifications. Immigration and emigration are issues directly related to the States, as any person arriving or leaving Australia on a permanent basis, must be domicile in a State, or Territory. The Commonwealth Government would have jurisdiction for the Territories, but each State would retain the authority to determine the level and type of immigrants they need, or can absorb. That level would be determined in conjunction with many diverse factors including emigration. The Commonwealth Government should determine, in agreement with the States, the standard criteria for accepting immigrants, but it must be up to the States to set the levels of immigration according to the needs and productivity of the State. Hence, as a Constitutional authority, this subsection should be qualified that immigration issues, at least, must be determined in conjunction with the States.

(*xxviii*) *the influx of criminals;* the anomaly relating to this subsection is the lack of definition for the word *"criminals"*. Seeing that Australia was founded on the back of imported *"criminals"*, were the *"founding fathers"* afraid that Britain might resort to deporting another batch of unwanted "misfits" from their English society? Technically, this responsibility only pertains to the Commonwealth in as far as the Commonwealth is responsible for Customs and Immigration at the ports of entry. The apprehension of "criminals" through any type of illegal entry essentially becomes a State matter. However, the Commonwealth Government should have the authority to deport any such *"criminals"*, but only after due process is served and they have been proven to be *"criminals"*. So again, we have a rather mindless subsection added to the Constitution, which gives the federal government a free hand to make all sorts of interpretations as to how they might apply this authority.

(xxix) *external affairs;* these two words represent two of the most dangerous words in this Constitution because, there is absolutely no limitations or indication, about how they should be interpreted. The ramification of these two words is so wide it can be, and has been used, to impact on domestic affairs that are internal to the Commonwealth.

External Affairs applies to the signing and agreement to treaties and various other forms of cooperation or collusion, with foreign organisations and governments. While benefits can accrue from some of these arrangements, virtually all of them involve some level of responsibility on the shoulders of the Australian people. Hence, any such treaty or agreement that becomes effective on the Australian population should have a Constitutional demand that it be approved by at least sixty percent of the combined Houses of Parliament before it can be enacted into Australian law. Although these *"external affairs"* arrangements are made by the political party in power at any given time, their impact can affect all Australians, and that is why a larger majority than fifty percent plus one should apply. This especially applies if any arrangement involves Australians being engaged in a foreign conflict. No government should have the authority to commit Australia to an overseas war without the significant support of a good majority of the people, especially if Australia is not under direct attack.

(xxx)   *the relations of the Commonwealth with the islands of the Pacific;* although this is an issue directly related to *"external affairs"*, for some strange reason it is treated as a separate issue. The fact that one *"external affairs"* issue can be treated this way raises the question why other more important issues, such as treaties and involvement in foreign wars, are not dealt with separately. Possibly, the answer to that question is that in 1900, the "foreign policy" of the Australian government was considered to be under the control of the British Parliament. In actual fact, that is the condition that applies to each of the British Colonies/Dominions that use the British monarch as their nominal "Head of State." At the 1911 Imperial Conference, when discussing an issue about treaties involving the Dominions, Sir Wilfred Laurier asserted that giving the Dominions the right to assent to a treaty was not an argument for separation, and Mr. Andrew Fisher, the then Prime Minister of Australia, agreed. The unquestionable proof that Australia's subservient status to Britain existed in 1914, especially in regard to "foreign policy", comes from the fact that King George V

declared war on behalf of the <u>British Dominion of Australia.</u>

(*xxxi*) *the acquisition of property on just terms from any State or person for any purpose in respect of which the Parliament has power to make laws;* although this is the proper ethical and moral responsibility of the Commonwealth Government, the subsection should specify the Constitutional provisions that allow that government to voluntarily, or otherwise, acquire someone else's property

(*xxxii*) *the control of railways with respect to transport for the naval and military purposes of the Commonwealth;* obviously, the States were not prepared to relinquish control of their state owned railways, but were prepared to allow the federal government a measure of temporary access for the single specific purpose of *"naval and military"* transport. Apparently, this was seen as a provisional requirement until the next subsection (xxxiii) could come into effect.

(*xxxiii*) *the acquisition, with the consent of a State, of any railways of the State on terms arranged between the Commonwealth and the State;* obviously, it was known that the various colonies used different gauges for their railway systems, and there would be a tremendous national benefit if all the systems could be converted to a standard gauge. That measure would have a significant impact on interstate trade and travel, and the subsection provides for this to be delegated as a federal responsibility. It was also recognised that this conversion would take a lengthy period of time before it could be successfully implemented.

(*xxxiv*) *railway construction and extension in any State with the consent of that State;* this follows on from the previous two subsections, but it does reinforce the concept of federation and the authority of the States to approve all issues relating to their railways.

(*xxxv*) *conciliation and arbitration for the prevention and settlement of industrial disputes extending beyond the limits of any one State;* again, it is obvious that the States intended to maintain control of their own internal industrial relations legislation, and were only prepared to limit the federal government's involvement to disputes that *"extended beyond the limits of any one State"*. That was probably fairly limited back in 1900, but this delegation has since proven to be very useful to the Commonwealth Government in a wide range of industrial issues, particularly when the Union movement became national.

(*xxxvi*) *matters in respect of which this Constitution makes provision until the Parliament otherwise provides;* in a strict legal and technical sense, this subsection virtually covers every contingency not provided for in the above subsections. In fact, it can be used to manipulate each of the above subsections by adding or subtracting from them in line with what *"Parliament otherwise provides"*.

(*xxxvii*) *matters referred to the Parliament of the Commonwealth by the Parliament or Parliaments of any State or States, but so that the law shall extend only to States by whose Parliaments the matter is referred, or which afterwards adopt the law;* while this is a fairly open ended provision because of the lack of definition for the word *"matters"*, there is a constraint by way of **Section 109** that gives the Commonwealth law precedence over any State law in the event of conflict.

(*xxxviii*) *the exercise within the Commonwealth, at the request or with the concurrence of the Parliaments of all the*

States directly concerned, of any power which can at the establishment of this Constitution be exercised only by the Parliament of the United Kingdom or by the Federal Council of Australasia; apparently, this subsection is included to convey complete autonomy to the federated colonies forming the Commonwealth of Australia. It is the basis for the enactment of the Westminster Act of 1942 and the subsequent Australia Act of 1986. The hypocrisy of the situation is that both these Acts had to be approved by the UK Parliament, and that makes a mockery of any concepts of autonomy. While this subsection applies to *"any power"* as *"exercised only by the Parliament of the United Kingdom or by the Federal Council of Australasia"* it does not apply to altering the federal Constitution, which both those above Acts attempt to do. As explained above in relation to subsection (xxii), if the government of Australia wanted to apply those Acts to the Constitution itself, they could only do that through the approval of the people via a referendum. No referendum has ever been held to legitimise either of those Acts, and hence, were Australia a nation truly governed by "rule of law", both Acts would be declared ultra vires.

As the State Constitutions have only limited and selective provisions for referendums, it could be argued that the UK Parliament does have the "power" to arbitrarily amend the State Constitutions, with or without the approval of the State Parliaments, let alone the people of the States.

(xxxix) matters incidental to the execution of any power vested by this Constitution in the Parliament or in either House thereof, or in the Government of the Commonwealth, or in the Federal Judicature, or in

any department or officer of the Commonwealth.
This is a totally obnoxious subsection by virtue
of its wide open generalities, and the deliberate
avoidance in applying any definitions. What are
"matters incidental"? Do they include major and
significant interpretations regarding the intent and
purpose of the Constitution, or does it mean minor
adjustments that are incidental in clarifying the
meaning?

Even the High Court of Australia does not understand the
meaning and intent of this subsection, as is confirmed from the
following extract from the Sue v Hill case of 1999.

*"Gaudron J: Under what head of legislative power was that
enacted?*

*Mr Bennett: **I suppose** 51 (xxxix), your Honour. It is incidental
to the nationhood power.*

*Gaudron J: **The nationhood power is implied**. There is no
51(xl), is there? Bennett: No your Honour there is not.*

*Gaudron J: Does 51 (xxxix) take you the distance? It is either
under the implied nationhood power or it is not, is it not?*

*Mr Bennett: Yes. Your Honour, Section 51(xxxix) can be read,
I suppose, as 'any power' as including any or all powers'.*

**It is rather awesome that the "nationhood" of Australia
can be considered as a *"matter incidental"* in the minds of
the High Court and the Attorney General. Clearly, the status
of Australia as a nation is a major issue involving every
Australian citizen.**

**The above exchange is a fine example of how the High
Court of Australia arrives at decisions derived from 'evidence'
based on supposition and implication.**

LESSON 12

There are nine remaining Sections to this Part V of the Constitution, which deals with the "Powers of the Parliament". In essence, they mop up anything that may have been overlooked in the substantive Section 51 and its thirtynine subsections.

Section 52 sets the tone for the remaining Sections, especially with the inclusion of subsection (iii), which reads, *"other matters declared by this Constitution to be within the exclusive power of the Parliament"*. It would be very difficult to define what *"matters"* are not exclusively declared by the Constitution, and obviously, the onus to provide such proof, and the cost thereof, would be on anyone contesting the Government's interpretation of this subsection.

Subsection (i) gives the Parliament the "power" to choose the location for the "seat of Government" and to make laws regarding, *"all places acquired by the Commonwealth for public purposes"*. Theoretically, the inclusion of the phrase *"subject to this Constitution"* means that subsection (xxxi) of the preceding **Section 51** will apply and any property would be acquired *"on just terms"*. That of course, does not mean the Commonwealth Government would not be able to simply requisition any property on any terms they deem appropriate.

Subsection (ii) of this **Section 52** introduces a new and undefined entity into the equation with its reference to *"the Executive Government of the Commonwealth"*. As we will find later in this Constitution, *"the Executive Government"* warrants its own Chapter II, exclusively to its existence and operation, but even that Chapter makes no sense in terms of the political reality in the way the government operates.

However, the initial wording of this subsection is somewhat ambiguous when it states *"matters relating to any department of the public service the control of which is by this Constitution transferred to the Executive Government of the Commonwealth"*. As there was no Commonwealth "public service" established at the time of the enactment of this British Constitution Act, does this provision give the Commonwealth Government the "power' to take over the relevant State public service infrastructure without any reference to compensation, or swearing an oath of office to the newly established Commonwealth?

Section 53 deals with the single exclusion that applies to the "powers" of the Senate in respect to the way that House deals with any proposed laws they are asked to approve. The exclusion is that the Senate cannot propose, or amend, any laws relating to *"appropriating revenue or moneys, or imposing taxation"*, but they can refuse to pass such laws and they can return them to the House of Representatives with proposals for amendment. It is then up to the lower House to accept or reject such proposals. It would be good if the Constitution were to explain the distinction between *"revenue and moneys"*, especially if *"revenue"* means "payment in kind", and if so, what is represented by "kind"?

However, as with so many things in the wording of this Constitution, there is a "funny" sentence added to the Section by way of, *"But a proposed law shall not be taken to appropriate revenue or moneys, or to impose taxation, by reason only of its containing provisions for the imposition or appropriation of fines or other pecuniary penalties, or for the demand or payment or appropriation of fees for licences, or fees for services under the proposed law"*.

The reason for including this sentence is not at all clear. Is this meant as an instruction to the House of Representatives that any law dealing with *"appropriating revenue or moneys, or imposing taxation*" must deal exclusively with those issues and not include any peripheral matters relating to *"fines, penalties and licence fees"*? On the other hand, is it a provision for the Senate to reject a "money" bill if those peripheral matters are included?

If this sentence is intended as an instruction to the House of Representatives, then surely this should come under a more appropriate section of the Constitution?

Section 54 deals with the question raised by that strange sentence in **Section 53**, which clarifies that *"The proposed law which appropriates revenue or moneys for the ordinary annual services of the Government shall deal only with such appropriation"*.

Section 55 actually goes a bit further than **Section 54** by differentiating between *"revenue or moneys for the ordinary annual services of the Government"* and *"Taxation"*. It seems there is some distinction between the two and *"Taxation"* is not to be used for *"the ordinary annual services of the Government"*. It even goes further still by differentiating between *"Taxation"* and *"duties of customs and duties of excise"* by stating that laws dealing with any of these three impositions must deal exclusively with each one separately, and if other things are included, the *"matter shall be of no effect."*

Once again, the wording of this section leaves something to be desired, as it confuses the distinction between *"laws"* and *"proposed laws"*, which is the subject of **Section 54**. A *"bill"* is a proposal for a *"law"* that is presented to Parliament, and it only becomes a *"law"* when it is passed by Parliament and given assent by the Governor General.

Section 56 is clearly a ludicrous provision by virtue it is never followed in practice under the Westminster system of Government. However, in terms of the way this Constitution is written, and particularly the overriding authority it gives the Governor General, it is logical that no bills for *"appropriating revenue or moneys"* should be allowed to pass *"unless the purpose of the appropriation has in the same session been recommended* *by message of the Governor-General to the House in which the proposal originated."*

It is curious that the phrase *"by message __of__ the Governor-General"* is used instead of *"by message __from__ the Governor-General".* Does this imply that the Prime Minister can write a *"message"* on behalf of the Governor General because; the Westminster system deems the Governor General a "lapdog" of the Prime Minister? (Except in the case of Sir John Kerr, who actually used the "powers" explicitly conferred on the Governor General in this Constitution)

Section 57 This Section is the one that resolves the question we raised earlier about the meaning of a *"double dissolution of Parliament".* When the Senate and the House of Representatives fail to agree on a bill after a number of attempts over a specified period of time, the Governor General can dissolve both Houses of Parliament and call for a conditional election. The condition being that an election cannot be help within six months of the expiry of the House of Representative's normal three year term. Here the "founding fathers" use the quaint expression *"effluxion of time",* which presumably means that if the House of Representatives has sat for thirty months of its three year term, an election has to be held off till the three year term expires. On the other hand, if the House has sat for less then thirty months, a double dissolution election can be held any time at the Governor General's discretion. Under **Section 12** of the Constitution, the writs have to be issued within ten days of the proclamation. In some respects, this Section could be seen as a contradiction to **Section 5** that only permits the Governor General to dissolve the House of Representatives. However, various anomalies seem to be part of the standard practice in creating this Constitution.

In the event of a double dissolution one presumes that all seats in both Houses are declared vacant, and the Senate has to go through the process of setting up the two classes of Senators as detailed in **Section 13**. The Constitution does not clarify this point, whether the group of Senators whose term is due to expire are the ones to become vacant, or if it means the whole of the Senate. Presumably, the Westminster system takes care of this anomaly as part of the unwritten "conventions" that permeate throughout that "system".

The remainder of the **Section 57** deals with an ongoing impasse after the proclaimed election. This allows the Governor General to call for a combined sitting of both Houses of Parliament, and have the impasse resolved with a majority vote, either for or against.

Section 58 spells out the authority of the Governor General to give assent, on behalf of the Queen, to any law passed by the Parliament, but it also gives the Governor General the authority to withhold assent at "his" discretion, or that "he" withholds the law for the Queen's pleasure. The *"founding fathers"* saw fit to throw in the meaningless expression *"but subject to this Constitution"*, and again, avoided specifying which sections of the Constitution should apply. Having now discovered **Section 51(xxxix)**, it would seem there is virtually nothing that is excluded as *"matters incidental"*, other than a *"matter"* that is specifically denied.

This **Section 58** also gives the Governor General the authority to propose amendments to the law and return it to Parliament for their deliberations.

The section is quite emphatic, and deals directly with the Queen of the UK as is proclaimed in Clause 2 of the British Act. And that is not withstanding anything implied by the change of the Queen's status under the Australian Parliament's 1973 Royal Styles and Titles Act, or the Australian Act of 1986, which only purports to deal with the UK Parliament and not the Queen per se.

The actual wording of the Section 58 is as follows:

58 Royal assent to Bills

"When a proposed law passed by both Houses of the Parliament is presented to the Governor-General for the Queen's assent, he shall

declare, according to his discretion, but subject to this Constitution, that he assents in the Queen's name, or that he withholds assent, or that he reserves the law for the Queen's pleasure.

Recommendations by Governor-General

The Governor-General may return to the house in which it originated any proposed law so presented to him, and may transmit therewith any amendments which he may recommend, and the Houses may deal with the recommendation".

The wording of this last sentence is almost identical to the wording contained in the US Constitution, but the US Constitution goes on to spell out precisely how such recommendations from their President must be dealt with. This British Act omits any such detail, as though the Governor General's recommendations are of little concern under the Westminster system.

Section 59 presents another hurdle to any aspiration the colony's Commonwealth Parliament may have as to their autonomy from the Royal authority. It gives the Monarch the authority to override any assent given by "her" Australian representative, the Governor General. The Monarch can do this at any time within a year of the Governor General's assent. As soon as the Governor General makes known the Queen's decision, the law is annulled and presumably stricken from the records.

There is no reference to any appeal or reinstatement of the law once the Queen disallows it. It is almost certain this provision was inserted by the British Parliament before they would agree to the Act being presented for consideration.

Section 60 deals with any law which the Governor General reserves for the Monarch's pleasure. The wording of this section is a little obscure; as it says the law will remain ultra vires for up to two years unless the Monarch gives assent within that period. What the section does not say is what happens to the law at the expiration of the two years, does it remain ultra vires, or can it come into force?

The logical assumption is that the law is annulled if assent is not received within the two years, but lawyers being lawyers, they tend to find meanings other than the logical ones.

For the clarity of the student, the actual wording is as follows:

Section60 Signification of Queen's pleasure on Bills reserved

A proposed law reserved for the Queen's pleasure shall not have any force unless and until within two years from the day on which it was presented to the Governor-General for the Queen's assent the Governor-General makes known, by speech or message to each of the Houses of the Parliament, or by Proclamation, that it has received the Queen's assent.

LESSON 13

Chapter II The Executive Government

This Chapter consists of ten sections and purports to explain how the government of this newly established Commonwealth of Australia is to function. This is as distinct from the Parliament described in the preceding Chapters. Supposedly, it deals with the day to day functioning of the bureaucracy, whose responsibility is to administer all the laws made by Parliament in relation to the various government departments. The Chapter defines which public service departments of the State governments are to be transferred to the Commonwealth Government. Some of these are to be transferred at a date determined by the Governor General, but the customs and excise departments of each State are to be automatically transferred at the establishment of the Commonwealth on the 1st of January 1901, when the British Act is proclaimed. The amalgamation the separate colonies into the federated colony to be know as the Commonwealth of Australia becomes official on that date.

As we will find, describing the way the Executive Government functions bears no relationship to what actually happens. The very first **Section 61** confirms the complete dictatorial "powers" that are vested in Queen Victoria (and according to Clause 2 of the Act, in her heirs and successors). Those "powers" are transferred to the Governor General as the Monarch's representative in Australia.

Section 61 reads: *Executive power: The executive power of the Commonwealth is vested in the Queen and is exercisable by* *the Governor-General as the Queen's representative, and extends to the execution and maintenance of this Constitution, and of the laws of the Commonwealth.*

Section 62 is a very curious Section. It reads: *Federal Executive Council: There shall be a Federal Executive Council to advise the Governor-General in the government of the Commonwealth, and the members of the Council shall be chosen and summoned by the Governor-General and sworn as Executive Councillors, and shall hold office during his pleasure.*

This highly mysterious body of people, to be known as a *"Federal Executive Council"*, is introduced in this Constitution without first defining anything about its makeup. There is no description of how many *"Councillors"* should be on this, seemingly, very important Council; how they are to be selected; or what tenure, if any, they should have, other than the Governor General's *"pleasure"*. The fact that the *"Councillors"* are only there *"to advise the Governor-General in the government of the Commonwealth"* reinforces his dictatorial status. There is nothing in the Constitution saying the Governor General has to act on that *"advice"*.

At this point, there is no reference to this *"Council"* having any links to the Parliament. Are we to assume it is a totally independent body, along the lines of the United States system where the President selects his own "Cabinet" outside of the elected members of Congress?

Section 63 attempts to clear up some confusing terminology, which we noted earlier in Section 32, and 33, when *"the Governor General in Council"* was used.

The Section reads: *Provisions referring to Governor-General: The provisions of this Constitution referring to the Governor-General in Council shall be construed as referring to the Governor-General acting with the advice of the Federal Executive Council.*

Again the term *"advice"* is used, but without any relevance to its standing, but it does clarify what is meant by *"the Governor-General in Council"*.

At last, **Section 64** throws some light on the makeup of this *"Federal Executive Council"*, but it is completely out of any logical sequence for explaining how the "Executive Government" is supposed to work.

The **Section 64** reads: *Ministers of State: The Governor-General may appoint officers to administer such departments of State of the Commonwealth as the Governor-General in Council may establish.*

Such officers shall hold office during the pleasure of the Governor-General. They shall be members of the Federal Executive Council, and shall be the Queen's Ministers of State for the Commonwealth.

Ministers to sit in Parliament

After the first general election no Minister of State shall hold office for a longer period than three months unless he is or becomes a senator or a member of the House of Representatives.

The Section deals with two scenarios, the first being the period prior to the first election of Parliament, and without specifically saying so, it "implies" the Governor General can create his initial *"Federal Executive Council"* in any manner and using any people he so chooses. These selected people were to be titled *"the Queen's Ministers of State for the Commonwealth"*.

However, after the first election to form the initial House of Representatives and the House of Senators, those chosen people could only remain on the *"Federal Executive Council"* for up to 3 months, unless they are elected to either Houses of Parliament.

This is a distinct difference from our assumption above that the *"Federal Executive Council"* could follow the US system of Executive Government. In fact, it conforms to the established British system, except, the Australian system, according to the Constitution, gives the total authority to the Governor General to select whom he wants to be his *"Ministers of State"*. This practice is not carried out under the Westminster system of Government and therefore, operates in direct contradiction to the Constitution.

Section 65 does at last; define the initial size of *"the Federal Executive Council".* It stipulates that membership should not exceed 7 people in total. The section does throw in two possible variations, one through the usual catch all phrase *"until Parliament otherwise provides",* and the other if *"Parliament"* cannot *"otherwise provide",* the Governor General can step in and *"direct"* the issue. Once again, the Constitution reinforces the powerful standing of the Governor General in respect to the Constitution.

The actual wording of this Section is as follows: *Number of Ministers: Until the Parliament otherwise provides, the Ministers of State shall not exceed seven in number, and shall hold such offices as the Parliament prescribes, or, in the absence of provision, as the Governor-General directs.*

A serious anomaly is created in this section by not specifying a minimum number of members necessary to form the Executive Council. Gough Whitlam and Lance Barnard allocated all the government ministries between them in December of 1972, and they went to the Governor General to form a constitutionally legitimate three man Executive Government (or dictatorship) of Australia. With the Governor General being the Commander in Chief of the Armed Forces, this would be a powerful alliance and entirely legal under this section of the Constitution.

Obviously, this Section needs to be considerably strengthened to prevent this situation happening again. Two provisions should be added to the section, first, in limiting ministerial portfolios to a maximum of two to any one Minister, and secondly, by specifying a **minimum** number of Ministers to sit on the Federal Executive Council, rather than a **maximum**, as in the current wording. Seven members would probably be a good **minimum**, but there should be no specific **maximum**, other than what is considered practical.

Under the Westminster system, it appears that the Ministerial positions are divided into classes, with a few of the more important ones forming the "inner Cabinet".

With the Westminster system reducing the role of the Governor General to that of a lackey to the Prime Minister, the actual functioning of the Federal Executive Council is nothing like what is spelled out in the Constitution. The operation of the Council is represented by a fortnightly meeting of one or two Ministers, and some Parliamentary Secretaries, to which it is not even necessary that the Governor General attend. Apparently, there is also a "convention" that anyone appointed to the Executive Council is appointed for life. So much for the "conventions" following the Constitution.

Section 66 is a curious one in terms of its ramifications. It reads: **Salaries of Ministers:** *There shall be payable to the Queen, out of the Consolidated Revenue Fund of the Commonwealth, for the salaries of the Ministers of State, an annual sum which, until the Parliament otherwise provides, shall not exceed twelve thousand pounds a year.*

By making the salaries for members of the *"the Federal Executive Council"* a direct responsibility of the Queen, rather than Parliament, and by implication, her representative, the Governor General, it makes the *"the Federal Executive Council"* a body answerable only to the Queen through the Governor General.

We can calculate that the twelve thousand pounds is to be distributed between the initial 7 Ministers of the Council, thus making each of their annual salaries around one thousand seven hundred and fortyone pounds. Bear in mind, the Governor General's salary at that time was ten thousand pounds a year, which clearly differentiates the importance of the Governor General in relation to any elected Member of Parliament.

We should also note that the annual one thousand seven hundred and fortyone pounds payable to Ministers of State is significantly more than the four hundred pounds payable to other members of Parliament specified in **Section 48**. As there is no mention of the Prime Minister in the Constitution, or as a member of the Federal Executive Council, one wonders how his remuneration is set, and whether it is determined by the Queen as defined in this **Section 66.**

The added clause *"until the Parliament otherwise provides"* does have merit in this case, as it takes into account inflation and any future increases in the number of members, even though it still represents an alteration to the Constitution. The Parliamentary condition only applies to the amount of money provided, and does not alter the procedure of paying the total to the Queen for disbursement. Is this procedure still being followed today?

Section 67 is another section that is completely out of its logical sequence, as it deals with the appointment and removal of *"officers"* before any provision is made for establishing which Public Service Departments will be part of the Commonwealth.

There is a welter of different terminology used in relation to this section, as it refers to *"**Civil Servants**"* in the title and *"officers"* in the actual text. **Section 69** talks about *"Department of the **Public service**"* and seems to differentiate between a *"Public Officer"* and a *"Civil Officer"*. Maybe this is just another case of "sloppy" drafting, and the terms are interchangeable?

For clarification, the Section reads: *Appointment of civil servants: Until the Parliament otherwise provides, the appointment and removal of all other officers of the Executive Government of the Commonwealth shall be vested in the Governor-General in Council, unless the appointment is delegated by the Governor-General in Council or by a law of the Commonwealth to some other authority.*

It is unclear why there is a doubling up on the conventional phrase *"Until the Parliament otherwise provides"* with the additional *"or by a law of the Commonwealth"*? Surely, any *"law of the Commonwealth"* can only come into existence through *"the Parliament"*, unless this is to "imply" that there are other laws that are automatically carried over after the Commonwealth is established. If this is the implication, then it opens up a whole can of worms in respect what those laws might be, and how many are involved. On the other hand, if this is just another case of "sloppy" drafting, and can be viewed as a meaningless addition, then it has no Constitutional effect. But as we know, lawyers love to home in on these sorts of technical aspects of legal documents; hence, the actual ramifications of this "doubling up" could be interpreted at the whim of any court chosen to hear a possible challenge.

Section 68 is the first unequivocal and straight forward section in this Chapter, as it clearly spells out the overriding "power" that backs up the office of the Governor General.

The Section reads: *Command of naval and military forces: The command in chief of the naval and military forces of the Commonwealth is vested in the Governor-General as the Queen's representative.*

It is well understood throughout history that there is only one "force" more powerful than any political or financial "force", and that is "Military force". Thus, as Commander in Chief of Australia's armed forces, the Governor General has the sole authority to implement a state of martial law should the circumstances warrant such an action. By any logical rationale, this authority would also carry over to the deployment of Australia's armed forces solely at the discretion of the Governor General. Under the wording of this Constitution, Parliament does not have any authority regarding the deployment of the armed forces, but would only have the opportunity to offer "advice" to the Commander in Chief through *"the Federal Executive Council"*.

Another glaring weakness with the Constitution is the absence of any reference to the Commonwealth becoming engaged in a war. The employment of Australia's military forces in any type of foreign conflict should only be allowed with the agreement of both Houses of Parliament, irrespective of the type of involvement. The one exception to this would be if Australia were to come under direct attack by foreign military forces, in which case, the Commander in Chief would

have the authority to act immediately, without going through Parliament

Section 69 finally comes clean as to what part of the Colonies/States infrastructure and public service departments are to be transferred to the Commonwealth.

The Section reads: *Transfer of certain departments: On a date or dates to be proclaimed by the Governor-General after the establishment of the Commonwealth the following departments of the public service in each State shall become transferred to the Commonwealth:*

> *posts, telegraphs, and telephones;*
> *naval and military defence;*
> *lighthouses, lightships, beacons, and buoys;*
> *quarantine.*

But the departments of customs and of excise in each State shall become transferred to the Commonwealth on its establishment.

The obvious reason for the immediate transfer of Customs and Excise is that they represent two of the principle means of raising revenue for the new Commonwealth. The other departments would be considered as ongoing expenditure commitments, and the longer they can be left as a responsibility of the Colonies/States the less burden they would be on the fledging Commonwealth's budget.

Section 70 is more or less a conventional "mop up" Section to try and cover any extraneous issues relating to the Executive Government that aren't directly addressed in Chapter II.

The "open slather" nature of this section is reinforced by the generalised wording of the last option, *"or in the authority exercising similar powers under the Commonwealth, as the case requires"*.

There are absolutely no limitations implied, or intended, by adding this option, as it can be read in any way the reader, the court, the bureaucrat, or the politicians choose to interpret its meaning. No Constitutional provisions should be written in this manner, especially as the ultimate impact would always be to the detriment of the people of Australia.

LESSON 14

Chapter 3 The Judicature

Chapter 3 is written in what appears to be conventional legal terminology, and while being largely devoid of definitions, it is apparently, quite clear to the legally trained mind. For any other readers, the original wording of the Chapter raises a multitude of questions. When a referendum was held in 1977 proposing to limit the ages for Federal Judges, but without specifying an age limit, this resulted in a very extensive and detailed alteration to **Section 72** of Chapter 3.

In comparison to the original wording of this **Section 72**, the greatly extended detail says a couple of things about the Constitution generally. It obviously implies that much of the original wording of the Constitution leaves a lot to be desired, especially in terms of definitions and clarification of intended meanings. It also shows that there is a general awareness of this, particularly by the people required to draft these amendments. The third thing it shows is the huge amount of "license" that is automatically assumed when drafting an amendment, based on a simple two line question asked at the referendum.

Understanding the meaning of words

There appears to be two reasons why the meaning of the words in a Constitution can be interpreted differently. The first possible reason is that the accepted legal interpretation, stemming from the Westminster system, gives words a different meaning to the usual English language definition.

For example, the use of the word "may" doesn't mean what it usually means. In the Westminster legal sense, "may" is often read as "shall", but this is dependent on the pragmatic contingencies that are applicable to the issue. In other words, the legal fraternity can interpret words in any way that best suits them.

The second possible reason is that the meaning of words used in the nineteenth century has changed over the last hundred years. It is this evolution in meanings that presents an obvious problem when the legal fraternity rely on precedent in arriving at a judicial decision.

In many cases the precedent relates to a different period in time, where the culture and conditions would be totally different from today. In a logical sense, precedent should not be used. It detracts from viewing any current situation in the light of the facts and conditions as they apply today. In fact, any precedent relating to a person currently on trial is inadmissible for that very reason - it taints objectivity of the decision. However, the legal profession is quite content to refer to previous judgments when arguing a case, especially if it relates to a technicality that has nothing to do with ethics, morality, or the truth.

The problems of communication

A problem does occur when it is assumed that "everyone" understands the same meaning of a word, or more particularly, a commonly used phrase. More often than not, people interpret words and phrases differently. This can occur from the context, it can occur from the tone of voice and it can occur in relation to the circumstances involved. Making the assumption that everyone is interpreting words the same way is a very common communication problem. It can lead to misconceptions, misunderstanding, and sometimes, even conflict. It is a special problem when translating from one language to another, but it can also be a significant problem between the professional use of words in comparison to the ordinary everyday understanding of the words. No better example can be used than the legal profession, which often uses words in a completely different way, and with a quite different meaning, to the way ordinary people commonly use the words. There are a number of implications in this. It insinuates that a legal document, or even a legal process, can only be understood by a legally trained person. Hence, it is commonly assumed that a person who chooses to defend themselves in a court of law has a fool for a client.

The legislative process

When it comes to drafting laws for presenting to politicians as legislation, those drafts are always written by legally trained people. Probably, the majority of politicians are not legally trained; hence, when presented with a draft document of many pages for enactment into law, they are often ill equipped to handle such a task. A more conscientious politician would probably resort to seeking professional advice, but unfortunately, that advice would most likely come from another legally trained person. Most politicians simply do as the party leaders dictate, and vote as they are told without any real examination of the documentation before them. It is very rare that a politician ever genuinely seeks the opinion of the people most affected by any proposed legislation. Certainly not by requesting a detailed examination of the draft material, as it would be read and understood by those affected people.

Of course, politicians do hold public forums on occasion, especially if a contentious issue is involved, but the outcome of such forums is always pre-determined in advance. Other than perhaps in some changes to minor detail, those forums have virtually no effect on the intended proposals. Invariably, such forums are conducted in generalities and seldom, if ever, closely examine the draft legislation in detail.

With the above background information in mind, we can now start our investigation of **Section 71**, the first section of Chapter 3.

As with many other sections in this Constitution document, it again provides Parliament with virtual open slather in a number of areas. The Section starts off with the statement, *"The judicial power of the Commonwealth shall be vested in a Federal Supreme Court, to be called the High Court of Australia, and in such other federal courts as the Parliament creates, and in such other courts as it invests with federal jurisdiction....."*

To start with, what is the reason for giving *"a Federal Supreme Court"* the specific title of *"the High Court of Australia"*? Surely, "THE *Federal Supreme Court"* would clearly identify it as a singular authoritive court for the Commonwealth? Is there some connotation about the word *"Federal"* that could imply the States should have a say in the make up of this *"Supreme Court"*? So, that's our first question – should the *"Supreme Court"* of Australia be a creature of the Commonwealth Parliament, or should it be a creature of the States? For example; wouldn't it be reasonable to consider having each of the States nominate a Justice to sit on this *"Supreme Court"*?

The remainder of this first sentence provides a lot of leeway for the Parliament to set up an unrestricted number of other *"federal courts"*, as well as, apparently, taking over any State Court it chooses to *"invests with federal jurisdiction"*.

This would seem to be a great deal of "power" granted to the Commonwealth Parliament, without any type of constitutional constraints on the way the "power" is used, or abused.

We then come to the last sentence of this **Section 71**, which reads; *"The High Court shall consist of a Chief Justice, and so many other Justices, not less than two, as the Parliament prescribes."*

This sentence introduces the position of a *"Chief Justice"*, but gives no explanation of how this position is filled, or what qualifications might be required of such a Judge. Nor is there any explanation anywhere else in this Chapter to indicate if there is any special authority attached to this position. This last sentence does specify that the original make up of the *"Supreme Court"* would have to, presumably, consist of a minimum of 3 Judges, the Chief Justice and two other Judges, but it is open to Parliament to decide if they want to include more Judges on the Court.

However, while the Section 71 does give the Parliament the authority to determine the number of Judges for this *"Supreme Court"* it does not specifically give Parliament the authority to appoint, or approve the appointment of the Judges.

Section 72 does deal with the appointment of the Justices to the High Court, and any other federal courts *"created"* by the Commonwealth Parliament. The section hands the appointment to the *Governor-General in Council"*, but it omits any instruction about how these Judges are to be selected, or what qualifications would be applicable.

The original **Section 72(ii)** says that Judges can be removed from the court only on the *"ground of proved misbehaviour or incapacity"* and only by the *"Governor-General in Council."* A third condition was added to **Section 72(ii)** as a result of the 1977 Referendum that set a retiring age for Judges. Until that referendum, a High Court Judge was appointed for life, apart from the original two exceptions. Under the Westminster system of Government, it is accepted that a Prime Minister has the "right" to select a High Court Judge to fill any vacancy. This provides the Prime Minister with the opportunity to "rig" the High Court by selecting a Judge compatible to the policies of the political party then in power. Obviously, life long appointments give a Prime Minister much less opportunity to "rig" the court in their favour, hence, in 1977 Malcolm Fraser got the OK from the Labour Party to propose the referendum to limit the age of every federal court Judge, which thereby included the High Court of Australia.

The 1977 Referendum

The question posed in the referendum was as follows: *It is proposed to alter the Constitution so as to provide for retiring ages for judges of federal courts.*

Do you approve the proposed law?

This was a completely deceptive question, as it avoided specifying a retirement age and it deflected attention away from the main target, the High Court.

The positive answer to this proposal resulted in a text of three hundred and thirty five words being added to **Section 72(ii)** of the Constitution, none of which was ever publicised prior to the referendum.

As usual, the amendments dealt with a number of other things apart from initially restricting the age limit to seventy years. As for the Prime Minister's hopes of rigging the High Court, this was dulled by excluding Judges from the provision if they were appointed prior to the referendum. The amendments did allow the Judges to resign from the Bench if they so wished, something that was not provided for originally. The amendments also allowed Parliament to vary the retirement age below the seventy years that is initially stipulated.

In an effort to try and supposedly cover all contingencies, the amendment concludes with this very poorly written, and very long sentence that is open to all sorts of interpretation: *"A reference in this section to the appointment of a Justice of the High Court or of a court created by the Parliament shall be read as including a reference to the appointment of a person who holds office as a Justice of the High Court or of a court created by the Parliament to another office of Justice of the same court having a different status or designation."*

Exactly what this last phrase, *"to another office of Justice of the same court having a different status or designation."* is supposed to mean, or how it is intended to apply, is quite obscure.

There is a third subsection to **Section 72** that stipulates that Parliament may fix the remuneration of the Judges *"but the remuneration shall not be diminished during their continuance in office".* The 1977 amendment did not alter this arrangement.

Section 73 In keeping with the rest of this Constitution, the Parliament is given a virtual blank cheque to control what the High court can and cannot do. The Constitution does this with the words *"with such exceptions and subject to such regulations as the Parliament prescribes..."* and this control covers *"appeals from all judgments, decrees, orders, and sentences:*

(i) *of any Justice or Justices exercising the original jurisdiction of the High Court;*

(ii) *of any other federal court, or court exercising federal jurisdiction; or of the Supreme Court of any State, or of any other court of any State from which at the establishment of the Commonwealth an appeal lies to the Queen in Council;*

(iii) *of the Inter-State Commission, but as to questions of law only;*

Again we come across undefined terms, such as, *"original jurisdiction"* and *"the Queen in Council"*; another mysterious entity that is not mentioned previously in this Constitution.

The other point with this subsection (ii) appears to give the Commonwealth Parliament a degree of control over the State Supreme Courts and *"any other court of any State"* but only to the limit of where *"an appeal lies to the Queen in Council".* Apparently, this entity, *"the Queen in Council"* is also known as the *"Privy Council",* which is a sort of British High Court made up of members of the House of Lords. Appeals to the Privy Council continued to exist after 1901 when the Constitution was enacted, but were supposedly extinguished by the Westminster Act of 1942, and finally buried by the Australia Act of 1986. Assuming that is, both those Acts were properly legitimate. In the eyes of the people, those Acts could not become effective until they were agreed at a nationwide referendum, irrespective of what the legal and political fraternity believes.

The Queen in Council

However, this section does impose a restriction on Parliament via the following passage: *"But no exception or regulation prescribed by the Parliament shall prevent the High Court from hearing and determining any appeal from the Supreme Court of a State in any matter in which at the establishment of the Commonwealth an appeal lies from such Supreme Court to the Queen in Council."*

The exact purpose of this sentence is unclear, as it seems to be inferring that an appeal to the High Court of Australia can replace an appeal to the *"the Queen in Council"*, but it doesn't actually say that, and it doesn't seem to deny a plaintiff from pursuing an appeal to the *"the Queen in Council"*, if they don't get satisfaction from the State Supreme Court, or the High Court. Is this simply a scam to add another financial hurdle in the path of a plaintiff trying to get justice, by making it more difficult and more expensive to reach the ultimate authority of *"the Queen in Council"*?

It appears the "founding fathers" were not entirely satisfied with introducing this hurdle into the process because, they subsequently passed authority back to Parliament to add more conditions and restrictions via this last sentence of the Section, *"Until the Parliament otherwise provides, the conditions of and restrictions on appeals to the Queen in Council from the Supreme Courts of the several States shall be applicable to appeals from them to the High Court.* While this is a direct interference with the jurisdiction of the State's Supreme Courts, it is restricted to issues involving appeals to *"the Queen in Council"* As mentioned above, it is not till 1986, with the enactment of the Australia Act that appeals to *"the Queen in Council"* are finally eliminated. (Assuming that is, that the Australia Act is not ultra vires because it was never put to a referendum in Australia)

Section 74

This Section seems to expound on the fear of the "founding fathers" in allowing access to *"the Queen in Council"*, as it hands over authority to the High Court to "certify" an appeal if they so choose. Seemingly, this section is mainly related to Constitutional disputes between the States and the Commonwealth, but it does throw in the sentence *"Except as provided in this section, this Constitution shall not impair any **right** which the Queen may be pleased to exercise by virtue of Her Royal prerogative to grant special leave of appeal from the High Court to Her Majesty in Council"*.

Once more we are confronted with a new undefined term *"by virtue of Her Royal prerogative"*, a term that is no where else explained in this Constitution.

However, the "founding fathers' were not to be thwarted by this exception because they sought to let Parliament override *"Her Royal prerogative"* by inserting: *"The Parliament may make laws limiting the matters in which such leave may be asked, but proposed laws containing any such limitation shall be reserved by the Governor-General for Her Majesty's pleasure.*

Possibly, this final condition, *"shall be reserved by the Governor-General for Her Majesty's pleasure"*, was inserted by the British Parliament before giving their approval to the Act. Effectively, that condition places a restriction on the aim of the Commonwealth Parliament in eliminating *"Her Royal prerogative"*.

Section 75

This section gives the High Court the authority to exercise *"original jurisdiction"* in five listed occasions, however, the section declines to identify what is meant by *"original jurisdiction"*. As the Constitution is seen as a legal document, and presumably only intended to be read and interpreted by legally trained people, the "founding fathers" saw no point in defining this legal terminology.

As it happens, *"original jurisdiction"* simply means the High Court can directly hear a case from one of the five listed issues, without it having to initially go before a lower court.

Those issues are as follows:

In all matters:

   (i)   *arising under any treaty;*

   (ii) *affecting consuls or other representatives of other countries;*

   (iii) *in which the Commonwealth, or a person suing or being sued on behalf of the Commonwealth, is a party;* (Apparently, this permitted the 1999 Sue v Hill case to go directly to the High Court, rather than a Court of Disputed Returns)

   (iv) *between States, or between residents of different States, or between a State and a resident of another State;*

   (v) *in which a writ of Mandamus or prohibition or an injunction is sought against an officer of the Commonwealth;*

A *"writ of Mandamus"* is another legal term that refers to the High Court issuing an order obliging a person, or an organisation, to perform an action that is required by law, but in this case the Court is restricted to dealing only with *"an officer of the Commonwealth"*.

Section 76

Gives the Parliament the authority to extend the High Court's access to *"original jurisdiction"* in four additional areas of potential dispute, namely:

(i) arising under this Constitution, or involving its
interpretation;

(ii) arising under any laws made by the Parliament;

(iii) of Admiralty and maritime jurisdiction;

(iv) relating to the same subject-matter claimed under
the laws of different States.

According to Quick and Garran, there is a small legal, but apparently significant distinction in the wording between **Section 75** and **Section 76** in the way these lists of issues are to be addressed.

Section 75 say the High Court has *"original jurisdiction"* **"in ALL matters"** but **Section 76** says it applies **"in ANY matter"**. Obviously, the distinction is very subtle, but it was brought up in the 1999 High Court case "Sue v Hill".

Technically, subsection (ii) provides open slather for the High Court to hear any case they so choose, as virtually every conflict of opinion will be derived from *"...laws made by the Parliament"*.

Section 77

This Section is confusing, as it starts off referring to the "matters" listed in **Sections 75** and **76** and giving the Commonwealth Parliament the "power" to make laws for *"(i) defining the jurisdiction of any federal court other than the High Court"*

Does this mean the Parliament can either allow, or prohibit, any other federal court from being involved in any of the "matters" listed in the above two sections?

The next subsection (ii) seems to branch off into an entirely different area that is purely related to the differences in jurisdiction between a federal court and the State courts. This subsection reads:

(ii) defining the extent to which the jurisdiction of any
federal court shall be exclusive of that which belongs
to or is invested in the courts of the States;

It is hard to read this subsection as dealing with the "matters" relating to *"original jurisdiction"* granted to the High Court.

The third subsection is even more confusing because, it appears to be repeating what has already been said in **Section 71** that the Parliament has the "power" of

(iii) investing any court of a State with federal jurisdiction.

Is there a distinction here, and is it inferring that these State Courts that are *"invested with federal jurisdiction"* also have *"original jurisdiction"*?

While all this might be clear and straight forward to the legally trained mind, it certainly isn't clear to the people, which this Constitution is designed to affect the most.

Section 78

Once more we have a Section that is totally confusing through the use of undefined legal terminology. What does the phrase *"matters within the limits of the judicial power"* actually mean? Overall, this is a very dangerous provision being granted to Parliament, especially from "the people's" point of view. It says: *"The Parliament may make laws conferring rights to proceed against the Commonwealth or a State in respect of matters within the limits of the judicial power".*

To start with, it doesn't say to whom these *"rights"* are being given. But what is more sinister, is the implication that it is within the Parliament's authority to say what *"rights"* may, or may not be, *"conferred".* Nor does it define whose *"judicial power"* the Section is talking about, nor what *"limits"* it is referring to.

It is interesting to note that this is only the fourth time the word "rights" have been mention in this Constitution document. The only other times were in Section 41, dealing with a voter's "right", then Section 51(xxii) when referring to

"parental rights", and in Section 74 in reference to the Queen's "right" to use *"Her Royal prerogative"*. The word "rights" is being used in a deliberately obscure manner in Section 78 by inferring "rights" only exist by virtue of the Parliament "conferring" them into existence. The only other time a "right" is mentioned is in Section 100, when it is declared that any resident has the "right" to the reasonable use of river water in their State.

As we know, "inference" and "supposition" are considered legitimate legal processes by the High Court. (See Section 51(xxxix) above)

Section 79

This Section allows the Parliament to determine how many Judges may sit on any court invested with federal jurisdiction. This is a rather peculiar provision, as it seems to allow "Parliament"; assumingly with the agreement of both House; to interfere with the judicial process. The wording of the Section reads: *"The federal jurisdiction of any court may be exercised by such number of judges as the Parliament prescribes"*.

Does this Section thereby contradict **Section 71** that specifies the minimum number of Judges to sit on the High Court?

Does it mean Parliament can instruct the High Court as to whether a case can be heard by less than the full court?

Or does this section mean the "Parliament" can define how many Judges must be appointed to hear any particular case brought before any federal court?

It seems incredible that our "founding fathers", all fully trained and experienced lawyers, could allow such an inconclusive and nebulous section such as this, to be included in a Constitution.

Subsection 77(i) saw fit to include the words *"other than the High Court"*, but this condition has been omitted from **Section**

79. Is there a reason for this, or is it just another case of "sloppy drafting"?

Section 80

This is the "trial by jury" section that has been greatly misunderstood by many people. The Section reads: *"The trial on indictment of any offence against any law of the Commonwealth shall be by jury, and every such trial shall be held in the State where the offence was committed, and if the offence was not committed within any State the trial shall be held at such place or places as the Parliament prescribes".*

Quite clearly, trial by jury only applies to offences against Commonwealth laws, but jury involvement is further restricted by virtue that the charge has to be by *"indictment"*. Various types of offences can be handled in other ways without having to issue an" *indictment"*.

Trial by jury in a State Court is entirely up to the State Government, or possibly in some cases, the State Constitution. Most States have been progressively eliminating trial by jury, except in some of the more serious capital offences.

The other interesting point about trial by jury is that a jury is required to reach a unanimous decision. Here we have, a group of ordinary people, usually without legal training or qualifications, being asked to arrive at a unanimous agreement. For some unknown reason, the seven members of the High Court of Australia, supposedly the best legal brains in the nation, are not similarly compelled to arrive at unanimous decisions. Why is that? Why are split decisions allowed? Why is it acceptable that such important deliberations of the High Court can hinge on the "opinion" of one Judge? Judges are supposed to make decisions on the basis of "legalism", but if unanimous decisions cannot be reached, then obviously, there is something wrong with the

way the law is written. The court then has a duty to point this out to the Parliament, and Parliament has a responsibility to correct the anomaly. A split court does not have the authority to make a ruling on the intent of a law because, such a ruling is obviously flawed, by virtue of the fact there are alternative viable opinions.

And that applies even if there is only one Judge in dissent.

LESSON 15

Finance and Trade

Chapter IV is the longest and most patently out of date Chapter of the Constitution. It should have been progressively up dated throughout the last century, but apart from two amendments, one in 1910 and another in 1929, nothing was done. It consists of twenty six sections, and was written in a day and age, and under a financial era that ceased to exist in 1971. During the eighteenth and nineteenth centuries, most of the world's currencies were linked to what was spuriously known as "the Gold Standard". In 1944, the USA initiated the Bretton Woods agreement that established the US dollar as the world's reserve currency. It carried a single promise that any foreign holdings of the US dollar could be converted to gold at a rate of $35 an ounce. This deceptive "Gold Standard" came to an end in 1971 when the cost of the Vietnam War caught up with the US. President Nixon was forced to renege on that last remaining promise because; the US simply did not have enough gold reserves to meet the demand. That decision in August 1971 ushered in a new standard of fiat currencies, based on a variable exchange rate determined from a group of the world's major currencies.

This completely changed all the financial parameters that applied under the now defunct "Gold Standard" system, a fact that most governments and economists, have yet to understand.

The Gold Standard Myth

As this Chapter is titled "Finance and Trade", we need to clarify some of the issues surrounding the financing of a government. Although this Chapter is actually about government finance, it doesn't really deal with the issue in any detail. In nineteenth century, most governments were controlled by the "Gold Standard" concept, but in truth the concept is quite a ridiculous idea. What it amounts to is that a nation's money supply should be restricted to the amount of physical gold it has stashed away in a vault. Over the past three hundred years at least, virtually no government has ever had enough gold, or been able to raise enough revenue from duties, excise and taxes, to cover their expenditure, particularly with the cost of ongoing colonisation and war mongering. To cover the shortfall the governments had to borrow "money' from the private sector, and one of the most popular ways to do this was to issue interest bearing bonds. But it is a funny thing about this "borrowed" money – mostly it doesn't exist, other than some figures in a bank account, or as is more common today, figures in a computer spreadsheet. These government bonds are mostly "bought" by means of an accounting transaction where figures are transferred to a government account and pieces of paper are received in exchange. Those pieces of paper are government bonds, which are really only backed by the government's "power" to impose taxation on their people, and to a lesser extent, the assumption the bonds were somehow backed by gold held by the government. These two facts make government bonds the most secure form of investment for the private sector.

The vast bulk of private sector "money" is created by the private banks using the government approved fractional reserve system. This allows the banks to create, via a book entry, ten or more times the amount of "money" they hold in their customer's accounts. Thus for every dollar a bank holds in deposit, it can create ten to twelve dollars to lend out at interest.

This system is well documented, and as Mayer Amschel Bauer Rothschild was reported to have said in 1791, '*Allow me to issue and control a nation's currency and I care not who makes its laws*'.

Under our present financial system, around ninetyseven percent of the 'money' in our society is created as credit from the private banks. The government creates the remaining three percent in the form of coins and paper notes. There is simply not enough physical money in the world today to cover the vast amount of "money" held in bank accounts. As is now patently clear, the present day financial system dominates the lives of so many people in so many countries, precisely for the reason explained by Rothschild, *"The few who understand the system, will either be so interested from its profits or so dependent on its favours, that there will be no opposition from that class."*

It has been this slavish worship of the "Gold Standard" over the centuries that have strangled most governments in a never ending spiral of debt to the private sector.

Of course, the private banks love this "Gold Standard Myth" and have done their utmost to see that the myth is perpetuated.

The maintenance of the "Gold Standard" myth is the reason gold prices are continually quoted today in published financial journals and shown on the TV. It perpetuates the myth that "money" is somehow officially tied to gold. No currencies in today's world are officially redeemable in gold. However, gold is still promoted as a "store of wealth", but in reality, gold itself is actually useless, unless it can be converted to either "money", or some other physical asset that is needed.

What alternatives are available?

Way back in 1861, President Lincoln had an alternative answer when he used the authority of his government to create the US money supply, known as the "greenbacks." His answer to the critics is the answer we should get from our politicians: *"The government should create issue and circulate all the currency <u>and credit</u> needed to satisfy the spending power of the government and the buying power of consumers..... The privilege of creating and issuing money is not only the supreme prerogative of Government, but it is the Government's greatest creative opportunity. By the adoption of these principles, the long-felt want for a uniform medium will be satisfied. The taxpayers will be saved immense sums of interest, discounts and exchanges. The financing of all public enterprises, the maintenance of stable government and ordered progress, and the conduct of the Treasury will become matters of practical administration. The people can and will be furnished with a currency as safe as their own government. Money will cease to be the master and become the servant of humanity. Democracy will rise superior to the money power."*

The "greenbacks" were the United States first and most highly successful step into the world of fiat currencies. Although "greenbacks" continued to legally circulate right up until 1994, they were finally phased out by the government, at the bequest of the Federal Reserve and the private banks.

A columnist in an 1865 edition of the London Times saw the threat of Lincoln's "greenbacks" and spelled out what needed to be done if the current financial system was to thwart the impending threat. He wrote:

"If this mischievous financial policy, which has its origin in North America, shall become endurated down to a fixture, then that Government will furnish its own money without cost. It will pay off debts and be without debt. It will have all the money necessary to carry on its commerce. It will become prosperous without precedent in the history of the world. The brains and wealth of all countries will go to North America. That country must be destroyed or it will destroy every monarchy on the globe."

The private bankers fought back by successfully getting the US Congress to pass a National Bank Act, and that Act eventually led to the formation of the Federal Reserve Bank in 1913. From that first Act and ever since, the US Government's money supply has been created as debt to the bankers who bought the US government bonds. It is this practice of setting up a Central Bank and issuing bonds that has since been adopted around the world. It simply perpetuates the need for Governments to borrow "money" and remain in the debt spiral.

The private banks continue to issue interest bearing credit to the private sector through the fractional reserve system. A relatively small amount of that "credit" is circulated in the form of legal tender, such as coins and notes, but there has never been enough legal tender available to cover a "run" on the banks. A major "run" happened in the 1930's, with the result many banks collapsed. Some governments resorted to uncontrolled note printing that was unrelated to the amount of goods and services available. That ultimately led to hyper-inflation, which has since been used as the deceitful excuse for preventing any government taking control of their nation's money supply.

No governments, then or since, have had the strength to rein in the power of the private banks that continue to dominate and control the economies of nations around the world.

The irrelevant and out of date Sections of Chapter IV

Having now explained some of the background to financing a government, we can begin our examination of Chapter IV.

The first thing we notice is that fourteen of the twenty six sections deal with the establishment of the Commonwealth and various periods up to ten years thereafter. No Government in the last hundred years has seen fit to rescind or modify these now irrelevant sections. Four sections deal with a now defunct Inter-

State Commission that was set up in 1912 and subsequently abolished in 1950. Again, no attempt has been made to update this feature of the Constitution.

We must also bear in mind that this Chapter of the Constitution was written before Income taxes existed. This is the reason the bulk of government revenue is related to the collection of custom duties and excise. Whenever there is a shortfall the revenue is topped up by borrowing from the private sector, namely, the banks. This is despite the fact that **Section 51(xii)** gives the new Commonwealth full monetary sovereignty to create all the needed *"currency, coinage, and legal tender"*. However, in that day and age, and even today, the concept of a nation's sovereignty to create their money supply is beyond the comprehension of most people, although, as explained above, certainly not the private bankers.

Section 81 states the obvious that *"All revenues or moneys raised or received by the Executive Government of the Commonwealth shall form one Consolidated Revenue Fund..."* but appropriated for purposes subject to the condition of *"the charges and liabilities imposed by this Constitution"*. It is somewhat unclear as to what the difference is between *"revenues"* and *"moneys"* unless *"revenues"* means payment in kind rather than cash.

Section 82 states that the cost of collecting and managing these *"revenues or moneys"* is to be considered the first expenditure to come out of the *"Consolidated Revenue Fund"*.

Section 83 creates another undefined entity in the form of a *"Treasury"*. Are we to assume that the *"Consolidated Revenue Fund"* and the *"Treasury"* is one and the same thing, or is the *"Consolidated Revenue Fund"* just a bookkeeping account that is kept and maintained by the *"Treasury"*?

While the **Section 83** correctly stipulates that *"no money can be spent by the Commonwealth unless approved by a law made by the Parliament"*, does the introduction of the *"Treasury"* imply the setting up of a whole new bureaucratic government department?

There is a further sentence in this section that is no longer relevant, as it allows the Governor General to act until *"the expiration of one month after the first meeting of the Parliament..."* The whole of that sentence should have been removed as part of a logical and routine updating of the Constitution, but such a process has never been instituted.

Section 84 is a lengthy explanation dealing with public officers who are transferred from a State department when it is taken over by the new Commonwealth Government. The section starts off by saying that any officer being transferred shall come under *"the control of the Executive Government of the Commonwealth"*. This strange beast, *"the Executive Government of the Commonwealth"* is defined in **Sections 61** and **62**, as *"the Governor General and his Federal Executive Council"* Logically, one would have thought these transferred officers would have come under the control of their respective Departmental Heads, but that is not how the Constitution is written.

Although the last lengthy sentence of this **Section 84** seems confusing, apparently, it refers to any individual State public officer whose transfer is approved separately from an automatic departmental transfer. Any such officer must be treated the same as officers involved in a departmental transfer.

It is noted that there is no reference to any of these *"public officers"* being called *"public servants"*, as is the title commonly used. The difference between a *"servant"* and an *"officer"* is very clear – one serves and the other commands.

The sentence reads:

"Any officer who is, at the establishment of the Commonwealth, in the public service of a State, and who is, by consent of the Governor of the State with the advice of the Executive Council thereof, transferred to the public service of the Commonwealth, shall have the same rights as if he had been an officer of a department transferred to the Commonwealth and were retained in the service of the Commonwealth".

Essentially, the whole of this **Section 84** is redundant, and should have been, either rescinded or updated.

Section 85 is also redundant, apart from the couple of obligations that applied to the transfer of State departments and their assets. If any of the obligations are still considered appropriate, and applicable, this section should also have been updated to reflect the current reality.

Section 86 is only applicable to *"the establishment of the Commonwealth"* and is no longer relevant.

Section 87 refers to a *"period of ten years after the establishment of the Commonwealth"*, but it does include the phrase *"and thereafter until the Parliament otherwise provides"*. This allows the Commonwealth to deduct whatever costs they want in relation to the collection of custom and excise revenue from the States.

Whatever balance remaining, if any, *"shall, in accordance with this Constitution, be paid to the several States, or applied towards the payment of interest on debts of the several States taken over by the Commonwealth"*.

The phrase *"in accordance with this Constitution"* appears to refer to **Section 89** as this section deals with refunds to the States up until uniform duties are implemented. As per usual, the "founders" provide no specific reference to which part of the Constitution is relevant.

Section 88 says uniform custom duties have to *"be imposed within two years after the establishment of the Commonwealth"*. As the two years is long gone, this section is now redundant. A modification of this section would be to demand that uniform custom duties, and probably several other revenue items, must always be applied throughout the Commonwealth. Such a statement would remove the opportunity for the Parliament to tamper with the principle of uniformity.

Section 89 This section deals exclusively with the two year period until uniform *"duties of customs"* are established, and hence, the entire section is also redundant.

However, there is an interesting observation in the wording of both **Section 88** and **89** in that they only refer to the *"duties of customs"* and omit any references to *"excise"*.

As *"excise"* is included in **Sections 86** and **87**, we must ask if there is any significance in this omission. Or is it just another example of "sloppy" wording?

Section 90 This section is in two parts, the first part confirms that the Commonwealth shall have the exclusive "power" to rule on all customs and excise duties once uniformity is established.

The second part is probably now redundant, as it confirms the States will lose all their authority in these matters, including offering any *"bounties"* except for any agreements made before the 30th of June 1898. Any such agreements still in operation would negate the redundancy of this part.

It is unclear as to why the Commonwealth Government should want to take control of any *"bounties"* which the States might wish to offer as inducement or encouragement in the field of trade and commerce. Surely the States are in a better position to determine how best to address this issue?

Section 91 is a partial contradiction of **Section 90**, as it emphatically prohibits the Commonwealth from preventing any State offering *"bounties"* for *"gold, silver, or other minerals"*. However, it does seem to imply that the *"the consent of both Houses of the Parliament of the Commonwealth"* is required if a State wanted to offer *"bounties"* *"on the production or export of goods"*.

There is no explanation given for this restriction, or why there should be any differentiation between *"minerals"* and *"goods"*. Any ordinary person would expect the reasoning to be included in the section. Possibly, the distinction arose from the fact that abundant gold had been found at Ballarat and Bendigo in Victoria and that State wanted to jealously guard their control of the resource.

Section 92 The first part of this section seems to be totally ludicrous because, it says, *"On the imposition of uniform duties* *of customs, trade, commerce, and intercourse among the States, whether by means of internal carriage or ocean navigation, shall be absolutely free".* But "free" of what? Free of any transportation costs? Free of any sort of Custom duties? Free of any sort of Government regulations?

This is quite a ridiculous sentence to be included in a Constitution without any attempt at clarification. The second part of the Section is really a confusing mish-mash of provisions. On one hand it differentiates between a colony and a State, as though both can, or do exist after federation. As we noted earlier, this same confusion is evident in **Clause 6** of the British Act. The confusing wording is as follows: *"into any State or into any Colony which, whilst the goods remain therein, becomes a State…".* There is no provision in this **Clause 9**, "The Constitution", or elsewhere in this British Act, for converting a colony to a State, but the ambiguous wording seems to imply there is a process somewhere in existence.

Essentially, this second part is redundant as it applies to *"goods imported before the imposition of uniform duties of customs…."* Once again, a reference to *"excise"* is omitted, as though there is some special reason why the same conditions shouldn't apply to revenue raised by *"excise"*?

Section 93 is largely redundant as the two subsections are intended to apply to the States only *"During the first five years after the imposition of uniform duties of customs…"*

Thereafter, *"until the Parliament otherwise provides"* comes into effect, and the Commonwealth Parliament is virtually given an "open cheque" to do whatever they like regarding *"duties of customs".* Again, there is no mention of *"excise".*

Section 94 gives the Parliament another free go, but only after the *"imposition of uniform duties of customs",* to handle any disbursement of *"surplus revenue"* to the States. Seeing there have been few, if any, governments in the last hundred years or so that have been capable of achieving any *"surplus revenue",* this section is obviously redundant. Any "profit" a government might try to make from their tax payers would go towards paying off the continual debt that is always a feature of government. However, there is no reason the Commonwealth should not reimburse the States should a genuine case of *"surplus revenue"* occur. Such an assurance should be written as part of the update to this section.

Section 95 is totally redundant as it deals specifically with Western Australia, *"if that State be an Original State"*, and only *"during the first five years after the imposition of uniform duties of customs"*. Western Australia appears to have flexibility in setting their rate of custom duty. There is no provision in this section for the Commonwealth Parliament to impose any other arrangement on Western Australia, either during or after the five years. However, as Western Australia was not classified as *"an Original State"*, it could be interpreted that none of the provisions in this section apply to Western Australia. That would be more a case of "sloppy" wording than one of intent. Irrespective, the section should be seen as redundant, unless Western Australia was to claim their absence of *"Original State"* status were grounds for secession from the Commonwealth?

Section 96 This section provides a pointless condition by stating *"During a period of ten years after the establishment of the Commonwealth"* the Parliament can offer financial assistance to the States, but *"thereafter until the Parliament otherwise provides"* it can continue to do so *"on such terms and conditions as the Parliament thinks fit"*.

Why the ten years was included doesn't make sense as there are no special conditions attached to that period.

Section 97 Once again we come across this confusion between a colony and a State, as though both existed when this British Act was proclaimed. As we have noted above, the conversion of the colonies into Statehood is not defined in this Act, and nor is there any reference to how this is supposed to happen.

Apart from that confusion, the remainder of the Section is equally confusing, as it starts off writing about revenue being *"reviewed and audited"*, and then refers to *"the expenditure of money on account of the Commonwealth in the State in the same manner as if the Commonwealth, or the Government or an officer of the Commonwealth, were mentioned whenever the Colony, or the Government or an officer of the Colony, is mentioned"*.

What this means probably doesn't matter because the Section starts off with the conventional loophole, *"Until the Parliament otherwise provides"*.

However, there is certainly a Constitutional responsibility on the part of the Commonwealth to ensure that all revenue raising is properly *"reviewed and audited"*, and such a requirement should be part and parcel of the update to this section.

Section 98 This very short section, is one of the most "powerful' sections in the whole of the Constitution as it links transportation to trade and commerce and greatly expands the initial scope of the provision in Section 51(i). Apart from the two restrictions contained in **Section 99** and **100,** it gives the Commonwealth Parliament virtually unrestricted authority over ALL *"trade and commerce"* in Australia, and also to the principle means of transportation as it then existed. The section reads: *"The power of the Parliament to make laws with respect to trade and commerce extends to navigation and shipping and to railways the property of any State.*

Unlike the provision of **Section 51(v)** where the "founding fathers" had the foresight to add *"and other like services"*, they omitted to do so in this instance, hence it is questionable whether road and air transport come under Commonwealth authority.

Section 99 does stipulate the restriction on the part of the Commonwealth Parliament that *"any law or regulation of trade, commerce, or revenue"* shall not give preference to any State over another.

Section 100 adds another restriction by preventing *"any law or regulation of trade, commerce"* from interfering with *"the right of a State or of the residents therein to the reasonable use of the waters of rivers for conservation or irrigation"*.

Once again we come across a number of undefined words. For example, how is *"reasonable use"* defined, and by whom? Similarly, what is meant by the word *"conservation"* in the way river water is used?

Does this section mean that the State governments have the "right" to privatise their water supply and force the people to pay for their drinking and household water usage?

Despite this prohibition on the Commonwealth Government from interfering with the State's river waters, the High Court of Australia overturned the Tasmanian government's plans to harness the Franklin River in their State. That decision was in direct contradiction to this **Section 100.**

Section 101 This Section sets up an *"Inter-State Commission with such powers of adjudication and administration as the Parliament deems necessary for the execution and maintenance, within the Commonwealth, of the provisions of this Constitution relating to trade and commerce, and of all laws made thereunder"*.

As we noted earlier in **Section 73(iii),** the Inter-State Commission was established in 1912, and as a result of a High Court appeal decision it was abolished in 1950. It was re-established in 1983 only to be absorbed into the Industry Commission in 1989.

As a result, this section should have been updated in 1989, or even in 1950 when the Constitution provision no longer applied.

Section 102 This gives the Commonwealth Parliament the authority to *"forbid"* any State from giving preferences or discriminating with respect to railways. This section is specific to railways, and it leaves it up to the Inter-State Commission to determine if a State action is just and/or reasonable.

As railways were the principle means of transport for trade and commerce, this section is now largely redundant, and made even more so by its reliance on the Inter-State Commission. Clearly this section needs to be properly updated to conform to the reality of today.

Section 103 This section should now be rescinded as it deals exclusively with the membership of the Inter-State Commission. Basically, there were three conditions that applied to the members (a) that they were appointed by the Governor General in Council (b) they held office for seven years, and (c) their remuneration was not to be reduced while they were in office.

As with so many other things in this Constitution, there is no indication of how many people were to make up this Commission, how they were selected, or what qualifications were required. Parliament appears only responsible for determining the "powers" of *"adjudication and administration"*, but the Constitution does not say anything about how this body is to be setup, where it is to be located, or what involvement the States would have. Obviously, the States would have had a strong vested interest in how this Commission operated, but the Constitution appears to totally ignore that interest.

Section 104 This section is similar to **Section 102** in that it relates specifically to railway rates being charged *"for the carriage of goods"*. Any dispute about the rates is handed over to the Inter-State Commission for adjudication.

As with **Section 102**, this one is also largely redundant in its present form and should be updated if it is to be retained.

Section 105 Prime Minister Deakin did see fit to update this section through a referendum in 1910 that gave him the approval to remove the words, *"as existing at the establishment of the Commonwealth"*. The section itself allows Parliament to take over the public debts of the States, or a proportion of the debts according to certain statistical conditions. The section then goes into some detail about handling the costs and interest payments, and how the States would cover that. By deleting the above words, the Commonwealth was permitted to become involved, and/or take over, any subsequent debts the States after 1901.

Section 105A Obviously, the deleted words in **Section 105** did not achieve what the Commonwealth wanted, hence Prime Minister Stanley Bruce called another referendum in 1928 to ask the question *"Do you approve of the proposed law for the alteration of the Constitution entitled 'Constitution Alteration (State Debts) 1928?"*

As per usual, this simplified, and generalised question, resulted in this completely new **Section 105A** being added to the Constitution. It wasn't till the following year that the six subsections, comprising some two hundred and twenty six additional words was finalised and inserted. Two subsections stand out. One is subsection (2) which represents an aspect of retrospectivity. Technically, the subsection appears unnecessary because, it is referring to agreements made between the Commonwealth and the States. The subsection reads: *"(2) The Parliament may make laws for validating any such agreement made before the commencement of this section".* Why would any such agreement require a law to be passed unless it is to impose a condition on the agreement that wasn't part of the original intention? Surely, such an agreement could be re-negotiated if the changes are beneficial to each party.

By allowing this aspect of retrospectivity into the Constitution it sets a precedent that could be used in other areas.

Would the referendum have succeeded had the people been told the ramifications in assenting to that simple question?

The subsection of major concern is subsection (5), and it seems to say that *"every such agreement"* is completely beyond the law of either the Commonwealth Constitution or the State Constitution. The subsection is totally ludicrous, and has absolutely no justification for inclusion in the Constitution. It reads: *"Every such agreement and any such variation thereof shall be binding upon the Commonwealth and the States parties thereto notwithstanding anything contained in this Constitution or the Constitution of the several States or in any law of the Parliament of the Commonwealth or of any State".*

There is no way the people of Australia would have agreed to the referendum if they knew this sort of provision was to be included in the Constitution. This provision is bordering on criminality, as it is the people of Australia who are ultimately responsible for any debts incurred by either the State Governments or the Commonwealth Government. This is even more alarming when it is realised that the debts are mainly between the Governments and the private bankers and investors, and those "lenders" are given total freedom from any law in Australia.

We should probably bear in mind that it was Prime Minister Stanley Bruce who was directly responsible for destroying the original Commonwealth Bank in 1923, and handing it over to the private banking cartels through the appointment of selected Board members.

LESSON 16

The Philosophical foundation of a Constitution

The fundamental problem with constitutions is that they are, whether we like it or not, an expression of the basic philosophy accepted by the people of a nation, willingly, or by default.

However, before we delve into this lesson we should clarify what we mean when we talk about philosophies. Essentially, a philosophy is really just a set of ideas, or concepts, related to the study of some particular issue. In our investigation, the issue is writing a constitution to set up a government for the Commonwealth of Australia. Because this constitution is *the most important piece of paper*" in everyone's life, we need to find out what basic ideas and concepts are used to create this document.

How did the "founding fathers" think? What were the principles they used to develop the system for governing Australia? Who is perceived as the "owners" of the constitution? The answer to these, and other questions, will define the philosophy underpinning the constitution.

Just what is the philosophic foundation of this nineteenth century British Act, which we still use as our Australian Constitution, as of 2015?

When we commenced our investigation into this British Parliamentary Act for the Constitution of Australia, part of our task was to try and determine the form this constitution takes, and the purpose it wants to achieve.

Analysing the British Act

In actual fact, there are two issues involved in the case of the British Act in question. One is to look at the British Act as a whole, because many people like to view **Clause 9**, *"The Constitution of the Commonwealth"*, as a stand alone section of the Act. Can such a separation be justified, and if so, what are the ramifications of this separation?

Always bear in mind that we are talking about the culture and mores of the nineteenth century. Most certainly, the stated aim of the British Parliament in that day and age was to provide an *indissoluble* federated colony of Australia that would always be considered part of the British Empire. The very word *"indissoluble"* represents a flaw in the creation of the Constitution because, that word assumes something lasts forever. We all know nothing lasts "forever", and this is particularly so where politics are involved.

Apart from the above aim, the British Act also had another purpose. That purpose is to ensure the federated colony of Australia would always remain under the auspices of the British monarchical system. The net result of these dual aims was to ensure the maintenance of the status quo for the British legal, political and social systems that were in place at the time the Act was proclaimed.

Virtually, every official statement confirms that separation from Britain was never conceived as the purpose for Federation. That is also confirmed from the Australian point of view, as per quotes from Sir Henry Parkes in 1891 right through to Andrew Fisher in 1914.

Clause 9 of the Act is the actual text of the constitution for the Commonwealth of Australia, and this is the second issue we need to look at. Can we determine if there is any incompatibility between the Act as a whole, and **Clause 9** as a separate document?

The form of the Constitution

In reality, there are only two forms in which constitutions can be created. The first, and most common form, is the constitution written by the "rulers" of the society, whether that is the government or some part of the "aristocracy", e.g., the Barons writing the Magna Carta. The second, and far less common form, is a constitution written *"by the people, of the people, and for the people"*.

In essence, the two forms are easily distinguished. The first form uses subterfuge in trying to claim a popular mandate from the society by using words, such as, *"Whereas the people ...."*

The second form of a constitution is clearly defined from the very first opening phrase, "We the people..."

The distinction between these two phrases is very pronounced. "Whereas the people..." obviously confirms that the "people" are presented with something, in this case a constitution, and theoretically are offered the choice to accept or reject the offer. This was the case for the referendums held in Australia in 1899 and 1990; where a certain number of qualified men were ask to choose between two options. In truth, the people weren't actually asked to accept or reject the constitution, they were asked if they wanted to federate the colonies or not; the acceptance of the draft constitution was thereby assumed if the vote was for federation. This is currently seen as a "democratic" process, but in the late nineteenth century, "democracy" was never a part of the political thinking, and the referendum idea was initially rejected by Queensland and Western Australia at the first attempt.

On the other hand, a constitution that starts with the phrase, "We the people..." firmly establishes who are the rightful owners of the constitution, and therefore, the true fountainhead of all political "power".

Perceptions

How the actual Constitution text is perceived can vary according to the views and perceptions of the reader. The British Act creating the Australian Constitution presents the quandary we mentioned above. Some people view **Clause 9** as a stand alone entity, and claim it represents the primary law for the newly created Commonwealth of Australia. Other people claim the complete British Act must be read in its entirety. This means that what is sometimes referred to as the "Preamble", must always be taken into account. There is no definitive "right" or "wrong" to either of these claims, and any stand taken can only ever be classed as an "opinion", irrespective whether it is based on precedent, history, or tradition.

The dual authorship of the British Act

As far as can be discovered, the purpose of the 1891 and 1897 Constitutional Conventions in Australia was to arrive at an agreement for the text of **Clause 9**; *"The Constitution of the Commonwealth"*. Who wrote the introductory paragraphs and the eight other clauses is unclear, but it would seem most probable that they were written, and included, as a natural part of the drafting process by the British law makers. If this is the case, we therefore have two separate groups of authors for the overall British Act.

It is also clear that most of the original participants involved in writing this **Clause 9** were lawyers and/or politicians. It is probably safe to say that the draft of **Clause 9** was always conceived as a legal document. This tends to be confirmed by Quick and Garran who wrote their monumental, "Annotated Constitution of the Commonwealth of Australia", and took one thousand and eight pages to try and define the legal implications of the document.

Our investigation to date has confirmed that the British law we currently use as Australia's Constitution is very much a colonial document from the nineteenth century. It displays the colonial attitudes of the era. In a political sense, this implies that the Westminster system of Government is to be adopted, even though there is absolutely no mention of this in the Act. The philosophy of the Westminster system is based on the use of unwritten conventions that allows the politicians, and their unelected party hierarchy, to adapt the system in favour of the political party in "power". Unfortunately, those attitudes are still retained today by every political party. The Westminster system is shrouded in the cloak of the monarchy. This is evident from the subservient attitude people hold towards the anachronistic monarchical system, even though the Queen has stated she has absolutely no authority over Australian affairs.

The British Act as it is actually written

If one reads the Constitution literally, it really sets up a totally dictatorial regime with the Governor General being Commander in Chief of the Armed Forces and given the power to assemble or prorogue Parliament at any time, plus withholding assent to legislation "at the Queen's pleasure".

This is not how a proper Democracy is supposed to work. But there again, Democracy was never part of the agenda for the "founding fathers".

As we have noted in earlier lessons, there is no mention of a Prime Minister in the constitution, nor any original mention of political parties, and it specifically states that it is the Governor General who selects his "Government in Council" (technically the cabinet, but in reality, something else) to "advise" him. Very little in the constitution works the way it is pronounced. The way Parliament and the government operate is based almost entirely on the code of unwritten "conventions", developed over the centuries by the politicians and lawyers to suit themselves.

All our "Founding Fathers" were completely aware of this, as they were aware of the effect of political parties and the powers and influence of a Prime Minister. They chose to ignore all of this and then write in thirtynine clauses allowing Parliament to change the constitution at their whim, and bypassing the need of going to the people.

Although the opening phrase of the American constitution starts with, "We the people...", it too was written largely by politicians and lawyers; all well versed in the established Westminster system of government inherited from Britain. Those authors too, used the sneaky underhand method of allowing Congress to amend the constitution, and like the Australian constitution, it has suffered ongoing manipulation over the years.

Until the Australian people wake up to this and decide they want a change - and more particularly – they want a say in developing this change – we will be left with the abortion of a document we currently have.

Morals and Ethics

People need to understand the basis of morality that has to be the foundation for any system, and they need to establish a viable code of ethics that recognises our individual responsibility to the society where we live. This can be done through a proper constitution that defines and limits the powers the society is prepared to allocate to any government **it decides to create**. That constitution must also give the people the power to recall, and dismiss, any member of the government who is proven to be corrupt, dishonest or incompetent.

Gary Weiss recently made the comment, "*Morality needs to become part of the national dialogue. We need to ponder our views and think more philosophically. We need to evaluate our own core values, and understand the moral foundations of social programs, and how they might be better implemented. Why is medical care available to the poor and elderly? Why is it beneficial to provide certain regulations for business? Why do paved roads represent a community benefit? Why should society provide and maintain parks or foster public education? Why is it beneficial for a society to have an informed and educated population that isn't restricted to people who can afford to pay for those services? Some people believe that society shouldn't do any of these things. Other people believe those institutions are a responsibility of a cooperative society, because, it's the right thing to do. It's right and natural to hold different concepts of right and wrong, provided those concepts are based on a morality and code of ethics that is acceptable to the society. It's a question of fundamental moral values, as defined by the society's traditions".*

Who owns the Constitution?

In the final analysis, the type of constitution that is adopted comes down to **who decides what is to be created.** Obviously, a trained and experienced lawyer is fully justified in writing a legal document. If a constitution is considered the primary law of a nation, who better qualified to write it than a lawyer?

On the other hand, if a constitution is seen as more than just the primary law, but also as an expression of how the people of a society wish to live their lives, then every interested person has a right, as well as a responsibility, to be part of the process.

In the case of the Constitution of Australia, it was wholly and solely written by the established colonial authorities of the nineteenth century, and the people were never given the opportunity to be part of the process.

Even today, the people still have no say in proposing any changes they may wish to make to this antiquated document. Under the unconstitutional and unwritten Westminster conventions, they are only allowed to pass judgement on a few changes that are endorsed by the political party system.

Rights and Principles

The above questions lead us into the subject of what PRINCIPLES should be enshrined in a constitution. Probably, the most important principle is to define the essential RIGHTS of every citizen in the society. In truth, there are only two essential rights – the right to a person's LIFE and their LIBERTY. If these two rights cannot be guaranteed and sustained, all other claims to "rights" are meaningless.

The other issue that must always coexist with any recognition of a person's individual "rights" is that all "rights" carry the responsibility not to infringe on anyone else's "rights".

Human nature guarantees that infringements will occur, and thus, it becomes a democratic government's principle responsibility to maintain the individual "rights" of each of its citizens, and address any infringements as they occur, but in accordance with the principles laid down in a constitution.

In terms of PRINCIPLES, and RIGHTS, another basic "right", but one subordinate to the above two essential "rights", is the "right to free speech". Virtually, every other claim to a subordinate "right" stems for this "right to free speech", because, if people are not allowed to express their ideas, their desires, their needs, and their solutions to issues, or the ability to voice their criticisms and dissent, then the concept of achieving anything for "the common good" is an impossible dream.

The concept of democracy stands or falls on the principle of the "right to free speech."

There are responsibilities that also go with this "right to free speech." It is another duty of a government to ensure this "right" is not abused by way of defamation and slander, inciting people to commit criminal acts, persecuting ethnic groups of any description, child pornography, and deliberately promoting falsified information. There are other limitations which might justify inclusion in this list, but it is up to the society to determine those limits.

Leadership

Within a society, history has shown there will always be people who aspire to be rulers. A society without a system of authority will quickly disintegrate; the people may scatter, and some will begin to fight between themselves. If he or she is an enlightened and wise ruler, then they can better deal with relationship problems within the society, and sometimes, even outside the society. A good authority system sets an example for future generations to follow. It can establish a set of rules which can make a society grow and prosper for the benefit of the future generations. When that authority becomes too authoritarian, corruption will set in. When the leaders begin to see themselves as rulers rather than servants of the people, when trade is done by compulsion rather than consent, when wheeling and dealing become accepted and work is demeaned, when honesty becomes self sacrifice, then society is on the wrong road and conflict becomes inevitable.

People are people, and the vast majority value their individuality and freedom to choose what they believe to be in their best interests. However, civilisations throughout history have always been controlled, either through the use of force and fear, or in more recent times, through their economy.

Over the last couple of hundred years, the development of democracy is the more prevalent political fad. This espouses the idea of individual freedom coupled to the concept of individual 'rights', but ties everything into an economy based on money. Under these circumstances, individual freedom cannot survive unless it is accompanied with economic freedom, and likewise, individual rights cannot be sustained, except by the economic wherewithal to defend them.

Every society will develop some form of leadership, but the trick is for the people of that society to have a non-violent way of controlling that leadership. In a democracy, rule of law seems a viable option, provided those laws conform to a philosophy that puts the protection of individual rights as a primary responsibility. Constitutions aren't just about the "law" - they have to be about "people", first and foremost. Whoever came up with the expression - "by the people, of the people and for the people" actually got it right.

This is where we have been misled – politicians/lawyers have almost always written constitutions, and a person can only be a lawyer if they are trained to think like a lawyer. That's why they can only see a constitution as a legal document.

A good constitution is also a philosophical document for how people want to live together as a society; setting up the rules is actually a secondary byproduct to setting up the principles under which all laws must conform.

We need rules because of human nature. Human nature comes in three basic forms - leaders, followers and non-followers. The leaders can be good or bad, but the followers are relatively easy to handle. It is with the non-followers that the problems lie.

Hence, a constitution for a society is really about dealing with the human nature of "people" - it is not about legal tradition, legal precedent, crime and punishment, it is about finding the best way a society can live together so that it will benefit everyone, followers and non-followers. It is a proven fact, that there will always be a form of authority in a society, and it is also a proven fact, that people will accept that authority if it is good for them. The trick is, not to make it 'bad' for the non-followers. If that can be done, the non-follower doesn't become disruptive. If they are free to follow their own path, they should be able to do that as long as it doesn't override the path of others.

And that is the fundamental issue of 'rights' and 'responsibility'.

LESSON 17

The States

Chapter V Again we are confronted with this apparent confusion as to whether the federation is a federation of colonies or of States, or even a combination of the two.

Why this ambiguity is allowed to exist seems quite unreasonable. Surely the "founding fathers" knew that the continent of the Australian mainland was divided into separate colonies as of 1897, plus the colony of Tasmania. Why then did they start referring to them as States in their constitution document while ignoring any transformation process that legitimises the change? And why did they keep using the phrase *"of a Colony which has become or becomes a State"*, which clearly implies the two entities existed at the time of federation?

In theory, it probably doesn't matter, as each partner of the Commonwealth is now accepted as being a State, or a Territory. However, the ambiguity is another example of the out dated nature of the constitution, and further reason why it should have been progressively amended over the years.

Section 106 This Section confirms that the existing constitutions of the States will continue in force, but subject to any provisions contained in the new British Act for the Commonwealth Constitution. The existence of some sort of process to convert a colony to a State is confirmed by virtue of the phrase *"or as at the admission or establishment of the State, as the case may be"*.

This wording indicates there are two processes involved in this conversion, one being the *"establishment"* of this new status, and the other being the *"admission"* into, presumably, the federation of the Commonwealth of Australia.

Again, there is no indication as to how these two processes are implemented.

Section 107 continues the same ambiguity in the opening sentence, by including the phrase *"of a Colony which has become or becomes a State"*, but **Section 107** refers to the "powers" of the Colony/State that will remain with them, unless, the Commonwealth Constitution specifically *"withdraws"* that "power" from the Colony/State Constitution. *"Withdraws"* is obviously the wrong word to use, as the Commonwealth Constitution does not give the Parliament any authority to tamper with a State Constitution. Besides that, it is the States who have agreed to relinquish certain of their "powers" to the federal system, as the Commonwealth could not have been created unless the States agreed. Consequently, the Commonwealth did not and could not, arbitrarily *"withdraw"* any power from the States.

Section 108 deals with the laws of a colony, by allowing them to remain in force after the colony is transformed into a State through our mystical and undefined process. The section itself is quite a convoluted and rather ambiguous paragraph, as it comes under the misleading subtitle: *"Saving of State laws"* The actual section reads: *"Every law in force in a Colony which has become or becomes a State, and relating to any matter within the powers of the Parliament of the Commonwealth, shall, subject to this Constitution, continue in force in the State; and, until provision is made in that behalf by the Parliament of the Commonwealth, the Parliament of the State shall have such powers of alteration and of repeal in respect of any such law as the Parliament of the Colony had until the Colony became a State"*.

This seems to mean that the Colony/State Parliament must *"alter or repeal"* any laws that don't conform to the requirements for converting from a Colony to a State?

Is this a further complication in the transformation of a Colony into a State that involves changes to the laws applicable to the different entities?

Section 109 This Section specifically gives priority to any Commonwealth law should a conflict arise with a State law. There is no reference to what applies in the case of a conflict with a Colony law. As strange as it may seem, the previous three sections imply that a Colony and a State can co-exist, but this Section only refers to a State. Why is this constitution so ambiguous?

The section reads: *"When a law of a State is inconsistent with a law of the Commonwealth, the latter shall prevail, and the former shall, to the extent of the inconsistency, be invalid".*

The reality of this situation seems to be that any State law remains in force until it is successfully challenged in a Commonwealth Court. There appears no practical process for reviewing the multitude of State laws to determine if a conflict exists. It is only when a dispute arises, and a legal challenge is mounted that the position can be resolved. Obviously it is in the State's interest to have any new laws reviewed for possible conflict, prior to submitting a bill to their Parliament.

Section 110 The section relates to the relationship between the State Governors, *"a Governor for the time being of the State, or other chief executive officer or administrator of the government of the State"*, all have to comply with *"the provisions of this Constitution"*.

As far as can be ascertained, there is only one other reference to a State Governor in this Constitution, and that is in Chapter 1 Part II, **Section 12**, which allows the Governor to cause a writ to be issued to fill a Senate vacancy. Why these other two "officers" have to be dragged into the constitution is a mystery. Can the States function without a Governor, and would a *"chief executive* *officer or administrator"* have the authority to assent to any State bills passed by their Parliaments? Every State operates through a Letters Patent provided by the Monarch, which authorises the Governor to act as the representative of the King or Queen, as the case may be. Only they have the authority to assent to bills and initiate them as State laws.

Section 111 provides for the Parliament of a State to *"surrender any part of the State"* to the Commonwealth, which will then have total jurisdiction if the surrender is accepted.

There is no mention of any compensation being involved in this *"surrender"* and nor are the people of the State given any say on the issue.

This section seems perilously devoid of any detail, both in terms of what constitutes *"a part"*, and why no compensation should apply.

Section 112 Once more we have an unusual use of the word *"produce"*. In particular, the words, *"net produce"* in this section renders the whole, lengthy sentence difficult to understand. On one hand, the section says the States can set up laws and charge fees for *"inspecting"* the import and export of goods for their State. Then it says: *"but the net produce of all charges so levied shall be for the use of the Commonwealth"*.

However, if we are to interpret the words *"net produce"* to mean *"the net proceeds"* or *"the net revenue"* then this seems to imply that the Commonwealth will closely examine the State's costs for carrying out inspections. Does the reference to *"net produce"* imply the State levy is expected to make a profit from their inspections?

If the word *"produce"* is read as it is normally understood to mean *"goods and products"* then the section doesn't make sense.

After giving the States permission to setup inspection laws, the section then says the Commonwealth has the authority to *"annul"* those laws, but doesn't require the Commonwealth to give a reason, or explanation, for any *"annulment"*.

As this section only applies *"After uniform duties of customs have been imposed"* it may mean that the Commonwealth has taken over all import and export inspections, in which case the section is redundant as it is written, and should be amended to reflect the current position.

Section 113 This section gives the States total control for making laws regarding *"All fermented, distilled, or other intoxicating liquids passing into any State or remaining therein for use, consumption, sale, or storage, shall be subject to the laws of the State as if such liquids had been produced in the State"*.

As *"excise"* is normally related to these particular products, it is curious as to why there is no mention of this revenue source in this section.

That raises the question as to what products are actually subject to *"excise"*, and the further question as to why *"excise"* is randomly used and omitted, as we noted in Chapter IV.

Section 114 This section deals with two disparate issues, but in a rather questionable manner. First, it says the States cannot *"raise or maintain any navel or military force"* unless the Commonwealth Parliament gives them permission to do so.

What is the reason for suggesting it might be OK for the States to have their own military forces? Perhaps this was seen as a stopgap measure in 1900, but the provision should no longer be relevant. As such, the wording of this part of the section should be updated.

The second issue raised in this section, but contained in the single long sentence, is that neither the State nor the Commonwealth, are allowed to impose any taxes on each others property.

Presumably, the reason for combining these two issues was in anticipation of the Commonwealth acquiring properties in each of the States for the purpose of military and navel establishments. As is usual with this constitution, there is a decided lack of explanation for many of the provisions it contains.

Section 115 This section is actually a quite powerful concession to the States, but one that is either not recognised, or never effectively utilised. The section reads: *"A State shall not coin money, nor make anything but gold and silver coin a legal tender in payment of debts"*.

There are a couple of anomalous issues with this statement, the first, it only prohibits the *"coining of money"* but does not include the *"issue of paper money"* or *"currencies"*, as mentioned in **Section 51(xii)** and **51(xiii)**. Are we correct in assuming the "Founders" considered there is a distinction between these three items?

The other anomaly is in requiring only *"gold and silver coins"* to be used in the payment of debts, but omitting to say where these "coins" come from, and who might be allowed to make them. It would also be interesting to know if any State, then or now, actually observes this constitutional instruction for the payment of their debts.

The exceptions regarding the *"issue of paper money"* could allow the State to create its own form of "greenbacks", as we discussed in the Chapter IV on Finance and Trade, for use within its boundaries. If those notes are backed by the physical assets of the State Government, and their issue is limited to an agreed percentage of the realisable value of those assets, the notes would represent completely "sound" money.

The section also represents a huge opportunity for an enterprising entrepreneur to create *"gold and silver coins"*, which the State is prohibited from doing. Such coins could transcend State boundaries, as their value would be recognised, and the requirement to use them for paying debts applies to all States.

It is an interesting concept worth pursuing.

However, as a result of some research, we find the "founding fathers" have actually plagiarised the US Constitution by using the exact words *"make anything but gold and silver coin a legal tender in payment of debts"*.

They have done this in apparent ignorance of the context for which the words were used in the US Constitution. By leaving out the reason for placing this prohibition on the States, the "founding fathers" have completely misconstrued the original intent, which was to counter the States issuing unrestricted "bills of credit". Too often those "bills" became an accepted media of exchange amongst the general public. In other words, the "bills of credit" became a form of "paper money", but unrelated to any type of proper controlling factors for their issue.

As the Australian Constitution completely misconstrues the purpose and intent for insisting on *"gold and silver coin"* being the only way a State can pay off its debts, the suggested interpretations above could be quite valid. The section as it is written would not prohibit the States, or a private concern, from acting in the manner proposed.

Section 116 This section only has an indirect relation to the States, other than every citizen in Australia has to live in one of the States, or a Territory. However, the section is actually quite poorly written, as it seems to prevent the Commonwealth from having any say in what defines a religious organisation, and its mode of practice. A lot of people consider this a declaration for religious freedom in the Commonwealth, but surely there has to be some criteria to define what can be classified as a "religion". Unless this is done, virtually any group could call themselves a "religious order" and be free of any government interference. For example, is Paganism or Devil Worship legitimate religions, and do they come under the wording of *"any religion"*?

The section reads: *"The Commonwealth shall not make any law for establishing any religion, or for imposing any religious observance,* ***or for prohibiting the free exercise of any religion,*** *and no religious test shall be required as a qualification for any office or public trust under the Commonwealth"*.

While this prohibition on making laws is in respect to the specified aspects of religious practice, it does not prohibit the

Commonwealth from making laws relating to religious issues outside of those specified aspects, e.g. religious education and religious schools, and exempting religious organisations from taxation.

Despite what many people like to assume, the Parliament does get involved in a wide range of issues relating to religions, especially when elections are due.

Section 117 This section is confirmation of Australia's continual subservient status to the British monarchy, which is actually the perpetuation of the long established feudalistic system that has been sustained for the past centuries of British history.

The section reads: *"A subject of the Queen, resident in any State, shall not be subject in any other State to any disability or discrimination which would not be equally applicable to him if he were a subject of the Queen resident in such other State".*

The wording actually says that *"disability or discrimination"* is permitted, as long as there is no difference as to how they are applied between the States. The section omits to say who is allowed to impose a *"disability"* on a *"Queen's subject"*, or by whom, and how, they can be discriminated against.

At the time of writing this section the majority of aborigines, if any, were not considered to be *"subjects of the Queen"* and neither too, were women, if the wording is read correctly.

While many people would consider this section redundant, it really cannot be excised or amended as long as the Queen reigns over Australia.

Section 118 This is a peculiar section, as it seems to cast a cloak of infallibility over State law making, and State *"judicial procedures".*

It is also strange in that it doesn't say who must give their *"full faith and credit"* to each of the specified actions of the States.

The Section reads: *"Full faith and credit shall be given, throughout the Commonwealth to the laws, the public Acts and records, and the judicial proceedings of every State".*

If this document is considered to be purely a legal document, for the exclusive use of the legal fraternity, then it probably means that they are the ones who are required to supply the *"full faith and credit"*. Clearly, they cannot do this if they are allowed to appeal a court decision, or to challenge a law made by a State.

On the other hand, if the Constitution is seen as a document of *"the people"*, as deceptively proclaimed in the very first words of the British Act, then the section is demanding, by virtue of the use of *"shall"*, that the people must accept anything the State does.

That is clearly ridiculous, but as the section does not impose any penalties on anyone who does not give their *"full faith and credit"* to *"the laws, the public Acts and records, and the judicial proceedings of every State"*, the section is fundamentally meaningless.

However, after some research we find this wording is taken directly from the US Constitution – BUT – the very important condition relating to the intent is left out. The missing words necessary to make sense of this section are contained in Professor Story's 1840 book. The words are, *"And the Congress may, by general laws, prescribe the manner, in which such acts, records, and proceedings shall be proved, and the effect thereof"*.

In other words, nothing can be taken in *"full faith and credit"* until it is certified and proven valid and applicable. So much for the astuteness of our "founding fathers" when they plagiarise only a part of the US Constitution, and clearly don't understand the significance of what they are plagiarising.

Section 119 We have a promise from the Commonwealth that they will protect every State from an invasion, but the last bit of the section does have to be read in terms of the nineteenth century terminology.

The Section reads: *"The Commonwealth shall protect every State against invasion and, on the application of the Executive Government of the State, against domestic violence"*.

Obviously, in today's parlance *"domestic violence"* has a completely different meaning to the nineteenth century interpretation.

However, this section does allow the Commonwealth Government to use the armed forces to quell any civil unrest that might arise from any issue. Effectively, it lays down the imposition of martial law, which in terms of the nineteenth century thinking, would have been a completely appropriate approach.

However, in the twenty first century, customs and expectations have changed, and this section needs to be fully amended to incorporate definite safeguards from allowing the Commander in Chief of Australia's armed forces to deploy his troops in civil disturbances.

Section 120 This section is the only one in this Chapter that does not raise a question. It is a logical and an appropriate provision, which the Commonwealth is prepared to share with, and assist the States. The section reads: *"Every State shall make provision for the detention in its prisons of persons accused or convicted of offences against the laws of the Commonwealth, and for the punishment of persons convicted of such offences, and the Parliament of the Commonwealth may make laws to give effect to this provision"*.

LESSON 18

New States

CHAPTER VI This is a relatively short Chapter comprising of four sections, but the title is a misnomer, as the Chapter also includes the adoption of new Territories.

Section 121 The section is far too broad and completely lacks any detail and conditions on how a new State might be established, particularly in relation to the existing States. The Parliament of the Commonwealth should not have the unilateral authority to create a new State unless it is in agreement with all the other States. Also, any new State must conform to the provisions and conditions set out in this constitution, and not to any special, or exclusive rules, *"as Parliament thinks fit"*.

The section reads: *"The Parliament may admit to the Commonwealth or establish new States, and may upon such admission or establishment make or impose such terms and conditions, including the extent of representation in either House of the Parliament, as it thinks fit"*.

No Territories should be converted to States unless agreed by all the existing States, and certainly, no existing State should be arbitrarily partitioned by the Commonwealth without at least, a State wide referendum of the existing State. Again, we come across this distinction between *"admission"* and *"establishment"* even though the logical sequence is reversed. Surely the *"establishment"* of a new State or Territory has to happen first before it can seek *"admission"* to the Commonwealth? There is an obvious paucity of details about how these two separate processes are to function.

Section 122 This section relates exclusively to Territories, and how the Parliament may deal with them, whether they are Territories handed over to the Commonwealth by a State, or given to the Commonwealth by the Queen, *"or otherwise acquired by the Commonwealth"*. Parliament is then allowed to grant representation to the Territory, *"in either House of Parliament"* under whatever terms it thinks fit.

It is this last condition that does not sit comfortably with the representation provisions laid down in the constitution for the States, as per Chapter 1 Part III **Section 24**. Representation should be related to the population of the Territories involved, and the constitution should be specific in saying that representation must be granted in both Houses of Parliament, and not *"in either House"* as Parliament *"thinks fit"*.

Section 123 This section allows the Parliament of the Commonwealth to alter the boundaries of any State, but only with the approval of the majority of the electors of the State, and the State Parliament.

This is actually a tricky provision because; if the area of a State is altered it must in some way, affect one or more adjacent States, unless it involves altering a Territory boundary. The section should have made provision for every State affected to have those electors, and those State Parliaments, approve the changes.

Section 124 At least this section conforms to the condition that should have been included in **Section 121**, The section reads: *"A new State may be formed by separation of territory from a State, but only with the consent of the Parliament thereof, and a new State may be formed by the union of two or more States or parts of States, but only with the consent of the Parliaments of the States affected"*.

The creation of a new State is really a national issue, as it has ramifications that affect all the other States in the Commonwealth.

At the very least, all the existing State Parliaments should approve, and a Territory Parliament if a Territory is involved. Ideally, the creation of a new State should gain the approval through a national referendum of all electors.

If such approval is gained then the conditions laid down in this constitution for the other States must apply to the newly formed State.

As this is a relatively short lesson, we are going to look at Chapter VII because, that Chapter only consists of two sections.

Miscellaneous

Chapter VII While this Chapter only consists of two sections, the second **Section 126** represents quite an alarming provision for a democratic nation. As we noted in earlier lessons, democracy was never a nineteenth century aim or intention for this constitution, however, in the twenty first century, most Australians definitely consider Australia to be democratic nation. Consequently, the **Section 126** should be either completely rescinded from the Constitution, or at the least, totally redrafted. A similar situation applies to **Section 125**, as it refers to establishing the seat of the Commonwealth Parliament, and as this has now been set up and the Territory of Canberra created, the section is redundant.

For the record, Section 125 reads: *"The seat of Government of the Commonwealth shall be determined by the Parliament, and shall be within territory which shall have been granted to or acquired by the Commonwealth, and shall be vested in and belong to the Commonwealth, and shall be in the State of New South Wales, and be distant not less than one hundred miles from Sydney.*

Such territory shall contain an area of not less than one hundred square miles, and such portion thereof as shall consist of Crown lands shall be granted to the Commonwealth without any payment there for.

The Parliament shall sit at Melbourne until it meets at the seat of Government".

Perhaps from a legal point of view, the section should be rewritten to confirm that the seat of government has been established in the granted territory of Canberra, as per the provision laid down in the constitution.

Section 126 is totally unacceptable in this day and age, if Australia is to be considered a democratic nation. We need to bear in mind that the Governor General is the Commander in Chief of the Armed Forces, and this Section allows him to appoint any number of *"Deputies"* he wishes, and to grant those *"Deputies"* whatever authority he chooses.

There is no provision for any of these *"Deputies"* to be approved, either by the people or the Parliament. This section would allow the Governor General to set up a central military command, and even declare martial law in Australia.

As the Governor General has the constitutional power to prorogue Parliament *"by Proclamation or otherwise,"* and *"in like manner dissolve the House of Representatives"*, (Chapter 1 Part I **Section 5**), this Section completes the total dictatorial powers granted by the constitution.

Again, for the record, the Section reads: *"The Queen may authorise the Governor-General to appoint any person, or any persons jointly or severally, to be his deputy or deputies within any part of the Commonwealth, and in that capacity to exercise during the pleasure of the Governor-General such powers and functions of the Governor-General as he thinks fit to assign to such deputy or deputies, subject to any limitations expressed or directions given by the Queen; but the appointment of such deputy or deputies shall not affect the exercise by the Governor-General himself of any power or function."*

As there is no provision in this constitution for anyone acting on behalf of the Governor General, should he be temporarily incapacitated, or otherwise absent, this section could be rewritten to reflect that situation, but only under strict limitations.

There was a **Section 127** in this Chapter, which expressed the racist attitude of the "founding fathers", and by implication, the people who supposedly voted for the draft constitution. In reality, the few eligible people were not asked to vote on the draft constitution at all, and they certainly didn't get asked to vote on the amended version passed by the British Parliament. However, the entire section was rescinded through Australia's most "successful" referendum in 1967, when the people were told about this objectionable provision.

The Section read: 127 Aborigines not to be counted in reckoning population

~~"In reckoning the numbers of people of the Commonwealth, or of a State or other part of the Commonwealth, aboriginal natives shall not be counted".~~

Having dealt with these two Sections, we shall now look at the final Chapter of the constitution.

Alteration of the Constitution

Chapter VIII This chapter consists of one long **Section 128**, and incorporates the concept of a nationwide referendum for changes to the constitution. Apparently, the concept is adapted from the Swiss practice, but certain significant differences have been applied.

While this section details how a referendum is conducted, and how the results are to be assessed, it says nothing about how proposals for alteration are to be initiated. But it does specifically lay down the way any proposal is to be presented to the people for their evaluation and consideration. It clearly says **_"the proposed law_ shall _be submitted..."_** – no ifs and no "buts" – the PROPOSED LAW must be submitted to the people – NOT a short abbreviated question for them to answer.

The only two conditions this section requires for a proposal to be put to referendum is that it *"must be passed by an absolute majority of each House of the Parliament, and not less than two nor more than six months after its passage through both Houses the proposed law shall be submitted in each State **and Territory** to the electors qualified to vote for the election of members of the House of Representatives"*.

The words *"**and Territory**"* were added as a result of one of the questions in the 1977 referendum being accepted by the people.

There is a lengthy portion of the Section that eventually allows the Governor General to step in if there is an unresolved dispute between the Houses about an alteration proposal. The Governor General is given the authority to *"submit <u>the proposed law</u> as last proposed by the first-mentioned House, and either with or without any amendments subsequently agreed to by both Houses, to the electors in each State **and Territory** qualified to vote for the election of the House of Representatives"*.

As we have pointed out above, there is a major problem with the way every past referendum has been conducted.

First, the alteration to be submitted to the people is defined as *"the proposed law"*, <u>which means the "law" as it is to be written, and to be included in the Constitution,</u> and that is what has to be presented to the people. Every government since federation has ignored this clear instruction, and deceitfully presented the people with a simplified question. The *"proposed law"* is never directly presented to the people prior to it being included. Mostly, the wording of the eventual "law" is never finally written or publicised, until the simplified question is approved.

This latter assertion is proven from the examples of the alteration to Section 15, (on casual vacancies for the Senate), and with Section 105A, which was inserted months after the referendum. It is obvious that Section 105A would never have been approved if the people were aware of what was to be included in this amendment.

A second problem arises by placing the Governor General directly in the political arena, and giving him the arbitrary "power" to make a political decision when Parliament cannot agree.

There is also a question as to why the Governor General should be allowed to intervene in the first place. Obviously, if agreement for an amendment proposal cannot be reached between the Houses of Parliament, there must be some serious reservations about its necessity or intent. No individual should have the power to override Parliament in this manner.

The third problem with this provision is that there are no conditions relating to the Governor General's timing for calling a referendum. As a nation wide referendum is an expensive exercise, it has been past practice to tie them in with a general election. This is done to reduce costs and reduce the alleged "inconvenience" to the electors by compelling them to give some thought to a constitutional matter.

Australia works on a system of compulsory voting, although this is not spelled out in the constitution, and this compulsion is enforced by fines if an elector does not vote.

In truth, this alleged "inconvenience" is not a big deal as there have only been nineteen referendums in the past hundred and fourteen years since proclamation of the British Act.

On top of that, the Act has some thirtynine provisions that allow Parliament to alter the constitution without going to referendum, and one of these provisions is even included in this section. It reads: *"When a proposed law is submitted to the electors the vote shall be **taken** in such manner as the Parliament prescribes"*.

Why Parliament should have the "power" to manipulate how votes are cast in a referendum, is both unexplained and unjustified. The constitution could have easily included a firm set of principles for casting votes. On the other hand, that provision could hinge on how the word *"taken"* is interpreted. Can it mean the way each individual vote is cast, or can it mean how the total vote(s) are used and applied?

The second part of this paragraph is now redundant, and should be either rescinded or rewritten. It reads: *"But until the qualification of electors of members of the House of Representatives becomes uniform throughout the Commonwealth, only one-half the electors voting for and against the proposed law shall be counted in any State in which adult suffrage prevails".* In the nineteenth century, females were not considered to be part of *"adult suffrage".*

Again we find the words *"a proposed law"* being used, and it now seriously questions the way the past referendums have been conducted. The above provision only gives Parliament discretion in how the vote shall be *"taken".* **It does not give the Parliament any discretion to ask simplified questions, or not present the full details of the *"proposed law"* to the people, exactly as it is to be altered, and/or inserted into the constitution.**

The next sentence in this section is the really specific condition in defining what is normally described by the government as a "successful" referendum.

The sentence reads: *"And if in a majority of the States a majority of the electors voting approve <u>the proposed law</u>, and if a majority of all the electors voting also approve <u>the proposed law</u>, it shall be presented to the Governor-General for the Queen's assent".*

How many more time does it need to be spelled out that the government must present *"the proposed law"* to the people whenever a referendum is called?

In the course of the nineteen referendums held over the past hundred and fourteen years, there have been fortyfour simplified questions put to the people. Of these fortyfour questions only nine of them have been "successfully" approved for the government. When we look at these fortyfour questions it becomes clear that the majority of them represent increasing the "power" of the federal Parliament, usually at the expense of the States, and almost invariably, at the expense of the people. The nine "successful" referendum questions did not appear to represent an increase in "power", but certainly on two occasions, the people were deceived when the details of the alterations were eventually added to the constitution. **(Section 51(xxvi)** and **Section 105A)**

The conventional "wisdom" likes to portray a "successful" referendum as a difficult exercise for any government, and this is because of the alleged "conservatism" of the people. However, if we look at referendums from the perspective of the people, we get a completely different picture. Rather than the people being "conservative", the "unsuccessful' referendums display a pronounced degree of "common sense". Effectively, they deny the federal government additional "powers" over the excessive "power" which that government already has, especially through the thirtynine alteration provisions incorporated into the constitution.

The penultimate sentence prevents a referendum being allowed to alter *"the proportionate representation of any State in either House of the Parliament, or the minimum number of representatives of a State in the House of Representatives...",* but the next part of this sentence is a bit obscure. It goes on to say: *"or increasing, diminishing, or otherwise altering the limits of the State, or in any manner affecting the provisions of the Constitution in relation thereto, shall become law unless the majority of the electors voting in that State approve the proposed law".*

Presumably, this means a nationwide referendum cannot alter the limits of any State, or any State laws, unless the people of the State concerned also agree.

The implication of this part of the sentence seems to say that the Commonwealth Government can propose changes to any particular State's territory, and/or its laws provided the majority of the other States and the majority of the voters, including the voters in the State concerned, do agree.

If the Commonwealth Government can do this to any one State, it means it can do it to every State, and that is a very broad authority to hand over to the Parliament.

State laws are already restricted by not being allowed to be in conflict with Commonwealth laws (Chapter V **Section 109**), and alteration to State boundaries is provided for in Chapter VI **Section 123**, so why is this provision necessary in **Section 128**?

The final sentence of **Section 128** was added as a result of a referendum in 1977, along with the words *"and Territory"*, as we noted above.

The sentence provides one of the few clear written definitions of an entity in this constitution. The sentence reads: *"In this section, Territory means any territory referred to in section one hundred and twenty-two of this Constitution in respect of which there is in force a law allowing its representation in the House of Representatives"*.

Although we have looked at the Oaths in **Section 42** above, in order to fully complete our investigation into the "piece of paper" Australia uses as its constitution, the prescribed Oaths of Allegiance and Affirmation, to which all politicians and Government officers are required to swear, are herewith repeated.

OATH of ALLEGIANCE

I, *A.B.*, do swear that I will be faithful and bear true allegiance to Her Majesty Queen Victoria, Her heirs and successors according to law. SO HELP ME GOD!

AFFIRMATION

I, *A.B.*, do solemnly and sincerely affirm and declare that I will be faithful and bear true allegiance to Her Majesty Queen Victoria, Her heirs and successors according to law.

(NOTE: *The name of the King or Queen of the United Kingdom of Great Britain and Ireland for the time being is to be substituted from time to time.*)

More detail of the points worth noting with these Oaths, are included in **Section 42**. Suffice to say, there has been no amendment made to include the fictitious Queen Elizabeth the II, Queen of Australia, and secondly, neither of these Oaths require the participants to recognise the people of Australia, or the Australian nation.

LESSON 19

The Westminster system of Government

The Westminster system of Government is a system that has been developed over the centuries within the British traditional and cultural heritage. That tradition and culture is very much a feudalistic one, where the general population is ruled by an aristocracy that derives its power and privilege from a long established monarchical system. The Westminster system itself relies, almost entirely, on unwritten and unrecorded conventions, none of which have ever been presented to the people for their approval.

Everything to do with the way the Australian Constitution is applied in practice, is based on this British "Westminster system" of government. Therefore, as good detectives, we must ask ourselves, "If this system has been around for centuries, why isn't it defined in the constitution?"

The only thing that seems to make any sense as to why it isn't included is that everyone involved with writing the draft, simply took it for granted. It was just assumed the government was going to operate that way, and it didn't occur to them to try and codify its practices.

There are a couple of facts that support our answer, the first being that the small group of people who were actually involved in drawing up the draft constitution, were mostly politicians or lawyers, all well versed in the system. The second fact is that the general public were never really part of the process, and they were never asked what type of government system they might have preferred. Obviously, a Republican system would never have been tolerated.

The above serves to answer another question, "Does this confirm that the founding fathers knew about the system?"

The answer is, "Of course they did. It was the only system they really knew, and it was the system that applied in all the Australian colonial governments of the nineteenth century".

So, what exactly is the "System" of Government in Australia?

Theoretically, there are three "systems" by which the Australian government can operate. The practice set out in the constitution is the first "system", but that one is largely ignored. There are a couple of exceptions, such as, having an Upper and Lower House in the form of the Senate and the House of Representatives. Another exception is requiring the Queen's assent, via her Australian representative, the Governor General, for any laws passed by the federal Parliament. The actual way Parliament works bears little resemblance to what is written in the constitution.

The second "system" is known as "responsible government", but it is more a theory than a "system". In days gone by, before the overriding influence of political parties, it used to be applied, more or less, as an understanding of the "right", or "proper" thing to do. Some politicians like to claim it is still being observed, but nowadays, that moral sense of ethical behaviour tends to be pretty much submerged in the swamp of party politics and peddled influence.

The third "system" is an adaption of the British Westminster "system" that our "founding fathers" planned to use for governing Australia, but without specifying the details in their draft constitution.

The First "system"

The first one is the "system" which we have studied in our lessons, and the one that is actually written in the British Act, with the constitution being included as **Clause 9**. As we have noted, this system is much more akin to a dictatorial system where the Governor General is the "Supreme" authority in Australia, and deriving all his "power" from the monarch of Great Britain. The system has nothing to do with "democracy", apart from a nineteenth century provision in giving some qualified male voters the opportunity to elect members to the House of Representatives and the House of Senators. Those qualified males were also allowed to cast a vote in a referendum, if and when the Parliament allowed one to occur.

In reality, this system is an agreement between the colonies of the nineteenth century, as to how they might share a certain proportion of their "powers" with a centralised government. In the eyes of the nineteenth century "leaders", these "powers" were the authority and responsibility to control the people.

The Second "system"

As we said above, the second "system" is largely a theoretical one that is referred to as "responsible government". In truth, its various "responsible actions" are only applied pragmatically, depending on the circumstances, and what the political party in power believes they can get away with.

Some of the "responsible actions" include a politician resigning if he or she is caught "deliberately" lying to Parliament. As "waffling", and telling less than the truth, is an essential characteristic for the political life, any "responsible action" relies on the interpretation of "deliberately". Of course, this can be difficult to prove, especially as no politician is infallible, and if they use information which they believe is given in "good faith", so be it. A good example is Colin Powell, telling the UN about Sadam Hussein having weapons of mass destruction; a completely false statement to justify the illegal invasion of Iraq, and the decade of destruction and chaos that followed.

There are numerous other "conditions" where "responsible government" is supposed to come into play; for example, when the Parliament passes a "no confident" vote against the government. Again, pragmatism becomes the principle criteria, just as it does when a government breaks a key promise made in an election campaign. The opposition always gets blamed on these occasions, and there is no way any government officer or politician, would be held accountable because they didn't do their "homework" properly.

In other words, there is never any direct accountability for broken promises, improper behaviour, or incompetent decision making, other than the three yearly elections.

In our every day society, individuals would normally be held directly responsible for their actions, but in the political arena, individual politicians are only responsible to their political party. If that party happens to be "in power", everything is done to paper over any threat of "responsibility" if it impacts on the party.

In past ages, when a person's honour was based on his word, or a shake of the hand, the theory of "responsible government" did carry some weight. With the advance of "litigation", and the ever present need to protect one's backside, "responsibility" is reduced to "crossing the "t's" and dotting the "i's". If there is a loophole in the system, the lawyers, and Judges, will exploit it for the benefit of their political masters.

The Third "system"

The third "system" is what is known as the Westminster "system". The version practiced in Great Britain has fundamental differences to the "system" that had to be adapted for Australia. England is not a federation of separate governments, as neither,

Scotland, Wales, Northern Ireland or any of the Channel Islands, were autonomous entities.

The British system consists of the House of Commons, which is currently made up of six hundred and fifty members, elected from around the nation. They are elected on the very questionable, "first past the post" system. This House is often referred to as "the lower House" because; the "upper House" is the House of Lords. That "upper House" is a purely hereditary one of unelected Lords, Peers, Archbishops, Bishops, and Law Lords, which now includes some twelve hundred people who are eligible to sit in this chamber. It used to have the power to reject Bills passed in the House of Commons, but in 1911, it was stripped of this power and can now only delay a Bill for various periods up to twelve months.

The House of Lords has been describes as *"a uniquely undemocratic, anachronism", and* its abolition, or wholesale reform, has been an ongoing drama for more than a century. The House of Commons is totally controlled by party politics, and to a lesser extent, so too is the House of Lords.

The Australian Adaption

The only significant resemblance to the Westminster system in the Australian Constitution, as it is written, is the establishment of an Upper and Lower House of Parliament, and the Queen's assent, through her Governor General, for the enactment of any laws passed by Parliament.

The "founding fathers" of the Australian Constitution were faced with an entirely different situation to the British scene, as they had five separate colonial governments to appease. Their answer was to adopt the United States system and establish a State's House to be called the Senate. The idea was to allow each State equal representation in the Senate, irrespective of the population of the State. In theory, the Senators were elected to represent their State, but as it turned out in reality, the members represent their political party. Mostly, the Senators towed the party line, irrespective of the impact on their State.

According to the Constitution, the House of Representatives is controlled by a member placed in the position of "Speaker", through some undefined process of being "chosen". A similar unexplained "choosing" process is used to install a President to be in charge of the Senate. Apart from these two identified positions, each without any details of their function, duties or authority, all other elected members are assumed to be of the same rank, unless they are appointed as department Ministers.

Despite the known existence of political parties, not only in the British parliamentary system, but also in each of the colonial Parliaments, there is no original mention of political parties in the Australian Constitution. This is quite extraordinary, because it is the Westminster system that endorses party politics, and that is what determines everything about the way the Parliamentary system actually works.

Australia's first Parliament

The constitution was corrupted from the very first attempt to form a government for the newly established Commonwealth of Australia. The first Governor General of the Commonwealth was the seventh Earl of Hopetoun, J.A L. Hope. He correctly chose the Premier of the federation's senior colony, New South Wales, to form a government. Sir William Lyne was offered the position of Prime Minister, despite the fact there is no such position in the constitution. Lyne's task was to form a cabinet, something that is also not named in the constitution, and arrange the first elections for the new nation.

As a result of some political manoeuvring by Barton and Deakin, et al, Lyne was unable to get sufficient support to form a cabinet. As a result, he had to return the commission to the

Governor General, and advise him to offer Edmund Barton the temporary appointment as Prime Minister. All this manoeuvring occurred in the latter months of 1900, even before the British Act was proclaimed.

Section 65 of the constitution stipulated that Ministers of State could not exceed seven, but Barton ignored that and collected nine of his political cronies to form this first temporary "cabinet." Barton and Deakin were the only two members of this first cabinet who had not been, or were, State Premiers.

This temporary cabinet did succeed in complying with **Section 5** of the constitution that required the first Parliament to sit within six months of the proclamation date. Elections were held around Australia on the twentyninth and thirtieth of March 1901, and the official opening of the first Australian Parliament was inaugurated on the ninth of May in the Melbourne Exhibition Building by the Duke of Cornwall and York, later to become King George V.

The Australian Westminster System

Everything about the Australian political system revolves around political parties, which were never mentioned in the original constitution. If a political party gets control of both houses of Parliament there is virtually no way of stopping them passing any legislation they want.

Under the Westminster's unwritten "convention", the Governor General becomes a lackey of the government, and does what he/she is told. While the constitution says he can take "advice", the Westminster system virtually demands he will take "instructions". The nebulous, and undefined, "Royal prerogative" is the only thing that stands in the way of this convention. The constitution says the Governor General can "select" people to be appointed to various positions, but in reality, he simply approves whomsoever the Prime Minister appoints.

The political party in power gets to form the government, and this allows them to load the public services and the judiciary with people compatible with the party's policies. Each government department comes under the control of a Minister, and while all the Ministers form the cabinet, there is a smaller group that forms what is known as the "inner cabinet". It is this "inner cabinet" that dictates the major policies of the government, often on the instructions of the unelected senior party officials. Although the Prime Minister is regarded as the leader of the party in the House of Parliament, he is not necessarily the President of the party, or in control of its executive body. All the ordinary politicians are known as "back benchers", and party discipline compels them to endorse whatever policies are put forward by their leaders. Mostly, they bow to this discipline under the threat or losing selection at the next election.

Parliamentary sessions are now televised, but it really only amounts to a form of "theatre" for the benefit of the general public, and usually quite childish theatre at that.

Virtually all the rules of parliamentary procedure are adopted directly from the Westminster system, and that includes all those unwritten conventions. The Speaker of the House of Representatives, as well as the President of the Senate, are given a wide range of authority, to limit discussion, to expel members, to rule on what is presented, to invoke standing orders, and even to play favourites, virtually without any accountability.

There are also a number of traditional and meaningless symbolic procedures used in the Australian Parliament that are copied from the British Parliament.

Checks and Balances in the Parliamentary system

Parliament is supposed to exist to scrutinise legislation, but the party in power minimises this scrutiny by curtailing debate. When a party has total control of both Houses of Parliament, they are in the position to rush bills through Parliament by using various tactics to avoid publicity and public awareness.

The primary concern of the Senate was originally intended to protect the interest of the States, but party politics put paid to that notion. Theoretically, the Senate provides a review mechanism that is seen as a way to introduce some checks and balances into the system. In actual fact, the only parliamentary safeguard the people have against tyrannical control by a few people sitting in the "inner cabinet" is when the political party holding the reins of government does not control the Senate.

The parliamentary system is also broken up into committees, where a few members get to look more closely at proposed legislation. While some of these committees are perceived as bipartisan, they invariably come under the control of the political party in power.

Thousands of pages of primary legislation come before parliament every year and there is even more pages of secondary legislation, all written in legalese, and mostly beyond the competence of any elected member to adequately scrutinise.

It can be even worse with money bills, as very few politicians have an accounting background, and even if they do, the amounts involved are completely beyond any experience they are likely to have handled.

Lobbying and Influence

Today's political system is really controlled by money. It takes a lot of money to run an election campaign, and the more money a party has available, the more advertising and TV time they can pay for. The actual membership of every political party in Australia is quite small, relative to the total population. It is not practical to rely on membership fees and member donations to fund an effective campaign, hence the evolvement of lobbyists. A lobbyist is a peddler of influence who sells his service to the highest bidder in order to get favourable treatment from the government.

Lobbyists are an ongoing fact of most political systems, and their clients are generally in the position to offer a financial incentive to benefit the political party. It is normally considered "corrupt" for any individual government official or parliamentarian to take a bribe, but that does not stop a political party from accepting a "donation". Of course, no firm commitments are ever given, up front anyway, other than some indication that the government may "look at" a particular issue, or perhaps consider the merits of a case at some time in the future. Thus, "corruption" is avoided on the vagueness of some verbal comments, which are almost never committed in writing.

The "revolving door" between parliamentarians and well paid positions in the private sector has become an established and accepted fact of political life. Thus, promises of a well placed career after one's "public" service in Parliament cannot help but influence the vote in the "right" direction. Even the substantial "retirement" and other benefits the politicians have awarded themselves on leaving office, pale against the incentives offered from certain organisations in the private sector. There are some proposals around to try and combat this overwhelming influence of lobbyists, but the benefits of the existing system are so great that change is akin to "flogging a dead horse".

LESSON 20

Elections

As the question of elections came up in Lesson 9, we should now look at the guidelines that ought to have been included in a constitution on how elections are conducted.

There are a number of different systems available, but probably the most crucial question is whether voting should be compulsory or optional?

Let's see if we can determine the pros and cons of this question.

Compulsory or optional voting

A democratic system is supposedly based on respect of the individual and "freedom" from coercion. These are supposed to be protected by a system of laws. However, any system of laws entails the existence of some form of "organisation", first to create the laws, then to administer them, and where necessary, enforce their compliance. In essence, that "organisation" is the government, and in a proper moral and democratic system, the laws are there for the universal application and assumed protection of everyone in the society. Unfortunately today, far too many laws are made for the benefit of special interest groups.

A government does not evolve out of nothing, and in a democracy, it should be the people of the society who create the government. Of course, governments can be created by dictators and tyrants, but in those cases any elections tend to be a farce, when freedom of choice is one of the first things to be eradicated.

As we have found, our government in Australia was set up by a relatively small group of people, based on their experience, heritage, training and familiarity with a system from the "mother country". It was specifically designed to maintain the status quo then in existence, which favoured the aristocratic and wealthy class of men over the more numerous male class of the Queen's subjects. Women and aborigines were virtually ignored, except for a few very limited examples in South Australia and Western Australia.

While democracy was never a serious consideration in forming the government of the Commonwealth of Australia, over the years, the principles of democracy have become a broadly accepted concept that most ordinary people in Australia take for granted. However, every government, democratic or otherwise, will always impose restrictions on the freedom of every individual within a given society. The distinction is in the degree of this restriction, and the fairness in how it is imposed.

From this point of view, every person in the society who is afforded the right to vote in elections has a direct responsibility for the type of government that takes up the reins of "power". And political "power" is nothing less than the "power" to control people. A government exerts this control by making innumerable laws to cover every aspect of life within the society.

The argument for compulsory voting

There are people who claim they have the right to choose whether to cast a vote at elections or not do so. In a totally free society that "right" would exist, but no such society exists, either now, in the past, or will do so in the future. Human nature guarantees that.

There will always be people who take the lead, and there will always be people who choose to follow a leader.

As we have pointed out above, the government of a society, and the laws it creates, affects everyone in that society. Hence, whether a person votes or not, they can directly or indirectly, determine the type of government that is empowered to control their lives, and everyone else's. By deliberately choosing not to vote they are defaulting on their responsibility to have a say in the choice of a government. It is the question of this "responsibility" that needs to be addressed when considering compulsory or optional voting. By not voting a person is offloading their "responsibility" for the type of government onto the shoulders of someone else. Does anyone have the "right" to expect someone else to carry that responsibility for them?

It's a matter of numbers

The choice between compulsory voting and non-compulsory voting really comes down to numbers. If one hundred percent of the eligible voters cast their vote, then there can be no question that the nation has decided on the preferred choices before them.

In a non-compulsory system, it would be logical to ask if there is some figure in respect to the votes cast that would confirm "the will of the people". There appears no objective way to determine such a number. If we say fiftyone percent of the eligible voters is the necessary minimum number for the votes cast, it is highly unlikely that all fiftyone percent would vote the same way. Consequently, an elected government would always represent a minority of the electorate as a whole. The same argument applies if an unlikely figure of eighty percent were chosen as the minimum participation. Again, the actual vote would be split, and the best case would be a fifty percent plus vote of the eighty percent cut-off, in favour of the government. That still leaves a potential fiftynine percent of the total eligible voters who either disapprove of the choice, or who couldn't care less. The other problem with setting a high number for authentication of a non-compulsory election would occur if that number was not achieved. Is the election then annulled, and another election called, or is the required number reduced to suit what ever result is obtained?

The very worst case scenario is when less than fifty percent of the eligible voters choose to participate. In that case, the only conclusion is that the people deserve whoever they get to control their lives and run their country.

The Argument against Compulsory Voting

The only really valid argument against compulsory voting is the specious claim of "freedom of choice". "Freedom of choice" is actually a strictly limited and proscribed "freedom" in any civilised society. Its application applies in a variety of areas, but every area has its accepted limitations. All governments impose restriction on the people they govern, but most people in a society would prefer those restrictions to be kept to a minimum. Similarly, the preference of most people is to have a government that consists of fair minded, honest, and ethical representatives. In the words of Professor Story, those representatives should *"be presumed to enjoy the public confidence and to be devoted to the public interest..."*. We might point out; there is a very distinct difference between *"the public interest"* compared to *"the party's interests"*.

For people who object to compulsory voting there is always the choice to cast an informal vote, and thereby render their vote meaningless. If the objection is against a penalty being imposed for not voting, surely it is not an unbearable imposition to ask a person to go to a polling booth once every three years, or so? There are postal vote options for people not conveniently close to a polling station.

As mentioned above, it really comes down to a matter of numbers, but the choice between compulsory voting and non-compulsory voting, should be left in the hands of the people to decide. However, the only really valid way to reach a decision on this would be to require compulsory voting at a referendum. That would provide a genuinely satisfactory resolution to the issue.

The matter of penalties for non-voting is another issue that could be reviewed. Are there any justifiable arguments for imposing a monetary fine for non-voting, or is conscientious objection a justifiable excuse? Certainly, imprisonment for any electoral offence should only be imposed as a last resort. Such action might apply if there is a proven case of deliberate fraud, slander, coercion or libel, involved.

Counting the Vote

Casting the vote is only one part of the electoral system; the more complex, and arguably important part, is the way the votes are counted.

There are several different systems in use for counting the votes, and each has their adherents, their advantages and their disadvantages. While the chosen system tends to be left in the hands of an elected government, it too, should really be a decision of the people. The only way such a decision could be obtained, is through a constitutional provision requiring the options be put to the people via a referendum.

In terms of the State elections, it doesn't matter if each State uses a different system, but whatever system is used should be the people's decision via a State referendum.

In the case of the national elections, there should be a single system in place for all the States and Territories, and again, that system should be decided by the people and not the government.

First past the Post

This system is somewhat satisfactory in a situation where one of the candidates gets more than fifty percent of the primary votes cast, irrespective of how many candidates contest the election. It is less satisfactory under a non-compulsory requirement. It is especially applicable if only two candidates are up for nomination.

It is far more acceptable if compulsory voting is required and the fifty percent minimum is obtained for any one candidate.

However, its significant weakness occurs when it is combined with non-compulsory voting, and multiple candidates available. Practice has shown it is very difficult of any one candidate to achieve the fifty percent minimum under these conditions. The question arises about the validity of a candidate's appointment when a clear majority of voters do not approve the choice? Is this a fair or logical system that properly reflects the "will of the people"? Although "first past the post" is the system used in the UK, it is not the system used in Australia.

The Preferential System

There are two options with the Preferential System. One option requires the voter to distribute his/her preferences between all the candidates standing, by numbering them in the order of preference. The other method is to allow optional preferential voting where the voter only gives their preference to those candidates he/she chooses, whether it's one candidate or more.

There is a sound argument for this latter option, as it does not force a voter to give his/her vote to another candidate whom they might otherwise oppose.

When no candidate achieves fifty percent plus of primary votes, the second preference is then counted, and added to the totals of the leading candidates. This process is repeated until one candidate ends up with the required fifty percent plus of the votes.

In theory, this is about as fair a system that can be devised, even though it can produce an outcome where a candidate with a majority of primary votes may not prove successful.

It has become standard practice in Australia to name each candidate according to their political party, and also to apply a system for the order in which the candidates are listed on the ballot paper. This listing system is often criticised, as it is claimed to contribute to the "donkey" vote; where the voter simply starts at the top, and numbers all the candidates from one down. There is no statistical evidence to verify the extent of this claim, or even its veracity.

However, the far more honest system for the ballot papers is to remove all connection to political parties, and simply list the candidates in alphabetical order according to their surnames. With two major political parties in Australian politics, and an Electoral Commission that clearly favours maintaining the two party system, removing party affiliations will not happen. It could be made to happen if a constitution provision were adopted in any future rewrite of the constitution.

Other Voting Systems

Tasmania and Canberra are the only two places in Australia that use, what is called, the Hare-Clark voting system. It is a semi compulsory system where a voter has to number all the candidates up to 5, if there are that many contesting the electorate, or they can number all of them if there are more than 5. The system then works on calculating a quota, which must be achieved for election to office. It is a more involved system than conventional preferential voting, but it has been used in Tasmania since 1909, with a modification in 1979. In some ways, the Hare-Clark system is a cross between proportional representation and the preferential systems.

The voting system adopted for the lower House in South Australia is called the "Instant Run-off Preferential system". This system involves eliminating candidates with the lowest number of primary votes and distributing their second preferences until one candidate achieves the fifty percent quota.

Victoria is the only State in Australia that has fixed Parliamentary terms of office. Their elections are always held on the last Saturday of November in every fourth year.

The preferential voting systems come under different names, such as, the Alternative vote, the Single Transferable Vote, the Hare Clark system, or the Instant Runoff system. Each system has its own rules and can be applied either optionally, or by compulsion.

Parliaments with two Houses

There are significant differences in the voting systems that apply to every parliament that consists of two Houses, as in some States and the federal Parliament. Most of the lower Houses are elected by a form of preferential voting, either optional or compulsory, while the upper Houses are mostly elected by a system of proportional representation.

The Proportional Representation System

Proportional Representation for the Senate was introduced in Australia by the Chiefly government in 1948, but it had first been unsuccessfully proposed in 1902 by the Barton government. There has been ongoing advocacy for its use, prompted in part by the Hare Clark system used in Tasmania, and an even earlier application, in 1840, at a South Australian municipal election

The proportional representation system is distinctly different from the preferential system used for the House of Representatives.

One of the principle differences is that each State, and each Territory, is treated as single electorates, thus complying with the original Constitutional intention of having the Senators represent their State. Territories were added later and were given Senate representation, but not on the same basis as in the original constitution for the States.

The intention of representing the State has been completely eliminated by the present day system favouring the party system. The voters are now given the choice to vote for either a political party, or to number each individual candidate according to the voter's preference.

The system is designed to elect members based on the proportion of votes they secure, as measured against a calculated quota. This quota is determined from a formula developed in 1868 by an English mathematician, Henry R. Droop, and it is still used today. The formula involves dividing the total number of formal votes, plus one, by the total number of positions to be filled, plus one. In a normal election today, where six Senators are elected, the quota of votes needed for election is fourteen point three percent of the total cast. That is reduced to seven point seven percent in the event of a double dissolution of Parliament. Surplus votes over the quota are passed onto the next preferred candidate, thus no vote is "wasted", as can occur in the preferential system.

Advantages of the Proportional Voting System

- It gives minor parties, and independents, an opportunity to be represented in Parliament.
- No votes are wasted as they are all eventually counted.
- The will of the electorate is better expressed, especially when there is dissatisfaction with the two party system that gives one party the control of the House of Representatives.
- The major advantage for the people is the potential for the minor parties to gain the balance of "power",

and thus force the governing party to moderate its legislation to better benefit the broader community.

Disadvantages of the Proportional Voting System

- The counting is a time-consuming process and can delay the final result.
- The disadvantage for the major parties is its threat of them losing control of the Senate, and thus the ability to force unpalatable legislation on the nation.

Review Requested:

If you loved this book, would you please provide
a review at Amazon.com?